Je, Tu, Nous

"These translations of Luce Irigaray's work will make a powerful contribution to feminist scholarship in philosophy, political theory, psychoanalysis, linguistics and poetics. Theorists of sexual difference will find a serious and subtle challenge in Irigaray's latest provocations."

Judith Butler

"Luce Irigaray is, arguably, the most original and provocative feminist theorist in contemporary French thought."

Elizabeth Grosz

Routledge Classics contains the very best of Routledge publishing over the past century or so, books that have, by popular consent, become established as classics in their field. Drawing on a fantastic heritage of innovative writing published by Routledge and its associated imprints, this series makes available in attractive, affordable form some of the most important works of modern times.

For a complete list of titles visit
www.routledge.com/classics

Luce
Irigaray

Je, Tu, Nous

Toward a culture of difference

with a personal note by the author
translated from the French by Alison Martin

 New York and London

The publishers gratefully acknowledge the assistance of the Ministère de la Culture in the preparation of this translation.

First published in English 1993 by Routledge

First published in Routledge Classics 2007
by Routledge
270 Madison Avenue, New York, NY 10016

Simultaneously published in the UK
by Routledge
2 Park Square, Milton Park, Abingdon, Oxon OX14 4RN

Routledge is an imprint of the Taylor & Francis Group, an informa business

Originally published in French as *Je, Tu, Nous* in 1990

by Editions Grasset & Fasquelle

© 1990 Editions Grasset & Fasquelle

Typeset in Joanna by RefineCatch Limited, Bungay, Suffolk
Printed and bound in Great Britain by
MPG Books Ltd, Bodmin

Library of Congress Cataloging-in-Publication Data
Irigaray, Luce.
  [Je, tu, nous. English]
  Je, tu, nous: toward a culture of difference: with a personal note by the author / Luce Irigaray; translated from the French by Alison Martin.— 1st Routledge Classics ed.
      p. cm.
  "First published in English 1993 by Routledge"—T.p. verso.
  Includes bibliographical references and index.
  1. Feminist theory.   2. Women—Social conditions.   I. Title.
HQ1190.I7513 2007
305.42—dc22   2006029611

British Library Cataloguing in Publication Data
A catalogue record for this book is available from the British Library

ISBN10: 0–415–77198–6
ISBN 13: 978–0–415–77198–6

CONTENTS

A PERSONAL NOTE

Equal or Different?

What woman has not read *The Second Sex*?[1] What woman hasn't found it inspiring? Hasn't as a result, perhaps, become a feminist? Simone de Beauvoir was indeed one of the first women in this century to remind us of the extent of women's exploitation, and to encourage every woman who had the good fortune to come across her book to feel less isolated and more certain about not being oppressed or letting herself be taken in.

So what did Simone de Beauvoir do? She gave an account of her own life while backing it up scientifically. She never

[1] Simone de Beauvoir, *The Second Sex*, trans. H. M. Parshley (Harmondsworth: Penguin, 1972), originally published as *Le Deuxième Sexe* (Paris: Gallimard, 1949).

1

stopped recounting it, bravely, at every stage. In so doing she helped many women—and men?—to be more free sexually, especially by offering them a sociocultural role model, acceptable at that time, of a woman's life, a teacher's life, a writer's life, and the life of a couple. I think she also helped them to situate themselves more objectively in relation to different moments in life.

Simone de Beauvoir did more. Her concern for social justice was a contributing factor in the support she gave to some feminists' actions, to their lives; in the ways she helped them gain social recognition by signing their petitions, by participating in their activities, encouraging the existence of a column for them in *Les Temps Modernes*, prefacing their books, taking part in their television programs, being their friend . . .

THE TIME OF PSYCHOANALYSIS

Although I read *The Second Sex*, I was never close to Simone de Beauvoir. Why? Was it because of the generation gap? It wasn't only that: she did associate with young women. That wasn't the issue, or not only that, anyway. There are important differences between our positions which, as far as friendship and mutual assistance goes, I had hoped could be overcome. In actual fact, they were not. When I sent her *Speculum*,[2] in which I wrote an inscription to her as if to an older sister, she never replied. I admit this saddened me. I was hoping for a careful and intelligent reading from her, a sister, who would help me with the academic and institutional problems I was having

[2] *Speculum of the Other Woman*, trans. Gillian C. Gill (Ithaca: Cornell University Press, 1985), originally published as *Speculum. De l'autre femme* (Paris: Minuit, 1974).

because of this book. Nothing came of this, unfortunately! The only gesture she made was to ask me for some information concerning *Le Langage des Déments*[3] when she was writing on old age. Not a word passed between us on women's liberation.

What can we make, then, of this distance kept up between two women who could, indeed should, have worked together? Aside from the fact that I had problems with academic institutions which are familiar to American feminists, for instance, but which were unknown to Simone de Beauvoir and which therefore she could not understand, there were several reasons for her reticence. Simone de Beauvoir and Jean-Paul Sartre were always wary of psychoanalysis. I am trained as a psychoanalyst and that's important (in spite of current practices and theories) for theorizing identity as sexual. I also have a background in philosophy, in which psychoanalysis takes its place as a stage in the understanding of the development of consciousness and History, particularly with reference to the sexed determinations of them.

Being educated in both of these fields has meant that my thought on women's liberation has gone beyond simply a quest for equality between the sexes. That doesn't stop me from joining and promoting public demonstrations for women to gain this or that right: the right to contraception, abortion, legal aid in cases of public or domestic violence, the right to freedom of expression—etc., demonstrations generally supported by feminists, even if they signify a right to difference.[4]

---

[3] *Le Langage des Déments* (Paris: Mouton, 1973).
[4] Nevertheless, my own position regarding jurisdiction is much more radical (see 10, "Why Define Sexed Rights?," p. 74).

3

However, in order that these struggles do not simply involve making demands, so that they lead to equivalent (but necessarily different) sexed rights being written into law, women—and couples too—must be allowed to accede to another identity. Women can only enjoy such rights if they find a value in being women and not just in being mothers. Which means that there are centuries of sociocultural values to be rethought, to be transformed. And that includes within oneself.

WOMEN: EQUAL OR DIFFERENT?

To demand equality as women is, it seems to me, a mistaken expression of a real objective. The demand to be equal pre-supposes a point of comparison. To whom or to what do women want to be equalized? To men? To a salary? To a public office? To what standard? Why not to themselves?

A rather more thorough analysis of the claims to equality shows that at the level of a superficial cultural critique, they are well founded, but that as a means of liberating women, they are utopian. Women's exploitation is based upon sexual difference; its solution will come only through sexual differ-ence. Certain modern tendencies, certain feminists of our time, make strident demands for sex to be neutralized. This neutralization, if it were possible, would mean the end of the human species. The human species is divided into *two genders* which ensure its production and reproduction. To wish to get rid of sexual difference is to call for a genocide more radical than any form of destruction there has ever been in History. What is important, on the other hand, is to define the values of belonging to a gender, valid for each of the two genders. It is vital that a culture of the sexual, as yet nonexistent, be elaborated, with each sex being respected. Owing to the cleavages in History in the gynocratic, matriarchal, patriarchal, phallocratic eras, the way we position ourselves sexually in our culture is related to generation, rather than to gender as being sexed. Which means that, within the family, a woman has to be mother and a man father, but we lack positive ethical values enabling both sexes of the same generation to form a creative, not merely procreative, couple. One of the main obstacles to the creation and recognition of such values is the more or less obscure hold patriarchal and phallocratic models have had for centuries over the whole of our civilization. It is quite simply a matter of social justice to balance out this power of the one sex over the other by giving, or giving back, cultural values to female sexuality. What's at stake is clearer today than when The Second Sex was written.

In bypassing this stage, feminism might well work toward the destruction of women, and more generally of all cultural values. In fact, egalitarianism sometimes expends a fair amount of energy denying certain positive values and getting nowhere. Which leads to the crises, disappointments, and periodic setbacks in women's liberation movements, and their failure to make a permanent mark in History.

Equality between men and women cannot be achieved without a theory of gender as sexed and a rewriting of the rights and obligations of each sex, qua different, in social rights and obligations.

Peoples never cease to divide themselves into secondary but deadly rivalries without realizing that their primary and insurmountable division is into two genders. In this respect, we are still in our cultural infancy. It's important for women's struggles, for women's social networks, and above all for each individual woman to realize the significance of the issues at stake which fall to them. Issues associated with the respect for life and culture, and with the continuous passage of the natural into the cultural, the spiritual into the natural. Women's responsibilities, their opportunities, have to do with a stage in world development and not some rather clear-cut and negative competition within a world undergoing transformation, where life itself is in many different ways in jeopardy.

To respect Simone de Beauvoir is to follow the theoretical and practical work for social justice that she carried out in her own way; it is to maintain the liberating horizons which she opened up for many women, and men. . . . She certainly found part of her inspiration for these during her long and often solitary walks in the countryside, in nature. It seems to me that her concern for and writings on this subject are a message not to be forgotten.

1

THE NEGLECT OF FEMALE GENEALOGIES

The question of sexed identity is one of the most important of our time. In my opinion, it's the most important, and for various reasons:

1. *Sexual difference is necessary for the continuation of our species*, not only because it constitutes the locus of procreation, but also because it's here that life is regenerated. The sexes regenerate one another aside from any question of reproduction. The latter might even weaken the life of the species by reducing sexual difference as such to genealogy. Some cultures have realized and acted upon this truth. More often than not we have overlooked it. Which has impoverished our sexuality, made it mechanistic, at times more regressive and depraved than animal sexuality, in spite of all our moral arguments.

2. *The status of sexual difference is obviously related to that of our culture and its languages.* Our centuries-old sexual economy is so often cut off from all aesthetic, speculative, and truly ethical elaboration that the idea of a sexed culture is astonishing to most people. Sex is said to be a matter separate from civilization. A degree of thought and enquiry will show that it's nothing of the sort; that sexuality, though said to be private, cannot possibly escape from social norms. And the fact that we have no or few specific sexual rules, rites, or ceremonies appropriate to our time simply reinforces this. During the development of our civilization the sexual order has been neglected. It's a sad irony that cultures as sophisticated as ours in many respects is should be so lacking or impoverished in others and should now seek sexual rules or secrets from animals, plants, and distant civilizations. What we need for our future civilization, for human maturity, is a sexed culture.

3. *The decline of sexual culture goes hand in hand with* the establishment of different values which are supposedly universal but turn out to entail *one part of humanity having a hold over the other,* here the world of men over that of women. This social and cultural injustice, which nowadays goes unrecognized, must be interpreted and modified so as to liberate our subjective potential in systems of exchange, in the means of communication and creation. In particular, it must be made apparent that we live in accordance with exclusively male genealogical systems. Our societies, made up half by men, half by women, stem from two genealogies and not one: mothers → daughters and fathers → sons (not to mention crossed genealogies: mothers → sons, fathers → daughters). Patriarchal power is organized by submitting one genealogy to the other. Thus, what is

---

now termed the oedipal structure as access to the cultural order is already structured within a single, masculine line of filiation which doesn't symbolize the woman's relation to her mother. Mother-daughter relationships in patrilinear societies are subordinated to relations between men.

FROM GODDESSES TO GODS

Societies other than patriarchal ones correlate to traditions in which there is a female cultural order, transmitted from mothers to daughters. Johann Jacob Bachofen, for example, outlines the basic characteristics of this female civilization in *Du règne de la, mère au patriarcat*.[1] I myself have analyzed certain events marking the transfer of the transmission of maternal-female power from the daughter to the son in *Amante marine*[2] (particularly in the chapters "*Quand naissent les dieux*" and "*Lèvres voilées*").

It should be pointed out that, with this transformation of spiritual genealogy, both the style and quality of the economy of discourse changed. Thus, in seizing hold of the oracle, of truth, the gods-men severed them from their earthly and corporeal roots. The change was accompanied by modifications in law, justice, and rhetoric. A new logical order was established, censuring women's speech and gradually making it inaudible.

Through incredible neglect and disregard, patriarchal traditions have wiped out traces of mother-daughter genealogies.

[1] Adrien Turel, *Myth, Religion and Mother Right*, trans. Ralph Mannheim (London: Routledge & Kegan Paul, 1968).

[2] *Marine Lover of Friedrich Nietzsche*, trans. Gillian C. Gill (New York: Columbia University Press, 1992), originally published as *Amante Marine* (Paris: Minuit, 1980).

9

Nowadays the majority of scientists claim, usually in good faith, that these have never existed except as a figment of the female or feminist imagination. Obviously, these scholars (men and women) haven't studied this question at length; they don't really know anything about it, yet they take the liberty of passing judgment according to the focus of their own research, without having sufficiently examined our cultural history. This neglect is symptomatic of patriarchal culture. It explains the dereliction and errancy of modern man, who knows nothing of the origins of his relations with the world.

HOW CAN WE DWELL ON EARTH WITHOUT GODDESSES?

In reference to this question, the French philosopher Jean-Joseph Goux, analyzes in a paper entitled "*L'oubli de Hestia*"[3] the nostalgic path Heidegger pursued in the quest for a possibility of dwelling on earth as mortals without renouncing the dimension of the divine as fulfillment and celebration. He explains that the term *Being* is often identified with the term *dwelling* in Heidegger's philosophy and that the coincidence of the two grows more marked as his thought progresses. To show this, Jean-Joseph Goux uses the Indo-European roots of these words. Now, these very same roots—signifying *Being* and *dwelling*—are related to the name of Hestia, the female divinity who guarded the flame of the domestic hearth. The divine is

[3] *Langages*, special issue: *Le sexe linguistique*, no. 85 (March 1987). This chapter is a revised version of the introduction I wrote for this collection of papers by Marie Mauxion, Patrizia Violi, Luisa Muraro, Marina Mizzau, Jean-Joseph Goux, Eliane Koskas, Hélène Rouch, and Luce Irigaray.

therefore watched over by the woman at home. It is transmitted from mother to daughter. When a daughter marries, the mother lights a torch at the altar of her own hearth, and, preceding the young couple, she carries it to their new residence. She thus lights the first fire of her daughter's domestic altar. The fire stands for the fact that the woman is the guardian of purity. Purity here does not signify defensive or prudish virginity, as some of our profane contemporaries might take it to mean, nor does it signify an allegiance to patriarchal culture and its definition of virginity as an exchange value between men; it signifies the woman's fidelity to her identity and female genealogy.[4] Respect for these female filiations and qualities attests to the sacred character of the home. The loss of the dimension of earthly inhabitance goes hand in hand with the neglect of Hestia in favor of the male gods, defined as celestial by philosophy from Plato onwards. These extraterrestrial gods would seem to have made us strangers to life on earth, which from then on has been thought of as an exile.

Such an interpretation of life on earth, the break with female genealogy, the disregard for its gods, its qualities, do nothing to bring about fulfillment in marriage, understood in the more general sense as the carnal and spiritual alliance between a man and a woman. However well a couple may get along, without a transformation of language and culture there can be no space for their intersubjective relations as a couple. The ensuing tragedies are often more evident in art and literature than in other forms of representation that are to a greater extent subject to the regulations of logical truth or the social

---

[4] At least this is the way I wished to interpret it. However, the privileging of fire and the later characteristic of this divinity are problematic. Unless what can be understood by it is a sort of memory of aboriginal traditions?

order, in which the artificial scission between private life and public life maintains a collusive silence on the disasters of loving relationships.

HOW SHE BECAME NOT-HE

The way culture has become patriarchal manifests itself, therefore, in the evolution of relations between the sexes. It is also marked in the deep economy of language. Grammatical gender is neither motiveless nor arbitrary. One need only do a synchronic and diachronic study of several languages in order to show that the distribution of grammatical gender is based on semantics, that it has a meaning related to our corporeal and sensory experience, that it varies according to time and place. So the same experience—if it's still permissible to talk like this, though to some extent sexual difference permits it—might be expressed by different grammatical genders depending on whether the culture, the moment in History, valorizes a sex or not. Sexual difference cannot therefore be reduced to a simple, extralinguistic fact of nature. It conditions language and is conditioned by it. It not only determines the system of pronouns, possessive adjectives, but also the gender of words and their division into grammatical classes: animate/inanimate, concrete/abstract, masculine/feminine, for example. It's situated at the junction of nature and culture. But patriarchal cultures have reduced the value of the feminine to such a degree that their reality and their description of the world are incorrect. Thus, instead of remaining a different gender, the feminine has become, in our languages, the nonmasculine, that is to say an abstract nonexistent reality. Just as an actual woman is often confined to the sexual domain in the strict sense of the term, so the feminine grammatical gender itself is made to disappear as subjective expression, and vocabulary associated with women often consists of slightly denigrating, if not insulting, terms which define her as an object in relation to the male subject. This accounts for the fact that women find it so difficult to speak and to be heard as women. They are excluded and denied by the patriarchal linguistic order. They cannot be women and speak in a sensible, coherent manner.

THE NEUTRAL AS LOSS OF IDENTITY

It is this untenable position in relation to discourse that causes most women who wish to have a say in culture to fall back on what they believe to be a neutral position. Yet this position is impossible in our languages. A woman denies her sex and gender in doing this. It's true that culture conditions her to do it. To behave in any other way, she must go through a complex and painful process, a real conversion to the female gender. This would seem to be the only way out of the loss of sexed subjective identity. Most women's experience tells them, on a cultural level, that they are first and foremost asexual or neuter, apart from when they are subjected to the norms of the sexual arena in the strict sense and to family stereotypes. The difficulties they face in order to enter the between-men cultural world lead almost all of them, including those who call themselves feminists, to renounce their female identity and relationships with other women, bringing them to an individual and collective impasse when it comes to communication. Culture, too, is considerably impoverished, reduced to a single pole of sexed identity.

The point of such thoughts, as well as those developed throughout this book, is certainly not just to denounce or criticize. They attempt to interpret the social structure with regard to its sexual order, or disorder. They also suggest specific tools for the analysis of this dimension and show, through examples taken from several important areas of current knowledge, that social justice cannot be achieved without a cultural transformation, the nature of which we can barely conceive.

Social injustice is due not only to economic inequalities in the strict sense. Our needs are not restricted to housing, clothing, and feeding ourselves. And what's more, I think it's a cultural distortion that leads to some people having a considerable amount of money whereas others do not. To invent currency was perhaps to create social disorder. In any case, our need first and foremost is for a right to human dignity for everyone. That means we need laws that valorize difference. Not all subjects are the same, nor equal, and it wouldn't be right for them to be so. That's particularly true for the sexes. Therefore, it's important to understand and modify the instruments of society and culture that regulate subjective and objective rights. Social justice, and especially sexual justice, cannot be achieved without changing the laws of language and the conceptions of truths and values structuring the social order. Changing the instruments of culture is just as important in the medium to long term as a redistribution of goods in the strict sense. You can't have one without the other.

March 1987

2

RELIGIOUS AND CIVIL MYTHS

Many of us are under the impression that all we have to do is not enter a church, refuse to practice the sacraments, and never read the sacred texts in order to be free from the influence of religion on our lives. In our countries, we have—at least in theory—a system that separates church from state, enabling us to maintain this illusion. Indeed, these measures taken to dissociate powers do testify to a relative degree of tolerance for the exercise of civil and religious passions. Nonetheless, this does not solve the problem of how significant is the influence of religion upon culture. Thus we are all imbued with the many Greek, Latin, Oriental, Jewish, and Christian traditions, at least, particularly through the art, philosophy, and myths we live by, exchange, and perpetuate, often without our realizing. The passage from one era to the next cannot be made simply by negating what already exists. The theories of Marx and Freud are not adequate, because they remain bound to a patriarchal mythology which hardly ever questions itself as such. Patriarchy, like the phallocracy that goes with it, are in part myths which, because they don't stand back to question themselves, take themselves to be the only order possible. That's why we tend to think of myths as representing secondary realities rather than as one of the principal expressions of what orders society at any given time.

HISTORY IN WORDS AND PICTURES

The disregard for what is termed, rather vaguely, Prehistory can be explained by the way in which patriarchy is mistaken for the only History possible. In examining Prehistory, specialists group very diverse facts and periods together and often reduce these historical expressions to the current function of myths (viewed as hidden in History) or that of fairy tales and legends. To consider the meaning of mythical representations of reality as merely incidental is concomitant to repressing and destroying certain cultural dimensions that relate to the economy of difference between the sexes. Such an approach also leads to a partial, reductive, and fruitless conception of History.

Johann Jacob Bachofen's work on myths as historical expressions[1] is interesting given the evidence he provides of the existence of gynocratic structures during particular eras. His findings are supported by various cultures that existed when ours were in their origins but that are closely related to ours. Gynocratic traditions—which should not be restricted to matriarchy but should include eras when women reigned as women—predate patriarchy but don't go back to the time

[1] *When God was a Woman* (New York: Harvester Press/HBJ, 1976).

16

of cave living, nor to the early paleolithic period, nor to certain forms of animal behavior as is interpreted and understood in supposedly knowledgeable circles. Thus, Greek, Roman, and Egyptian cultures all provide us with examples as cited by Bachofen (see too his bibliography and Merlin Stone's in *When God Was a Woman*) and by others—notably Herodotus, Hegel, and Eliade—not to mention the evolution of myths and tragedies, especially Greek ones, of which we have written traces. Aside from texts, there are numerous artistic remains in the strict sense that attest to aboriginal cultures different from our current civilization, cultures we have inherited, though not without censoring and inverting values. These values re-emerge from time to time through patriarchal norms.

DIVINE WOMEN

In May 1984, after a conference at the Venice-Mestre Women's Center entitled *Divine Women*,[2] I went to visit Torcello island. In the museum there is a statue of a woman who resembles Mary, Jesus's mother, sitting with the child before her on her knee, facing the observer. I was admiring this beautiful wooden sculpture when I noticed that this Jesus was a girl! That had a very significant effect on me, one of jubilation—mental and physical. I felt freed from the tensions of that cultural truth-imperative which is also practiced in art: a virgin-mother woman and her son depicted as the models of redemption we should believe in. Standing before this statue representing Mary and her mother, Anne, I felt once again at ease and joyous, in touch with my body, my emotions, and my history as a woman. I had before me an aesthetic and

[2] Cf. *Sexes et Parentés* (Paris: Minuit, 1987).

17

ethical figure that I need to be able to live without contempt for my incarnation, for that of my mother and other women. I also saw, at the church of Madonna dell'Orto in Venice, a picture of Mary as an adolescent arriving at the temple for her instruction and, in Bologna, at San Stefano, a small chapel dedicated to a Virgin child, which, judging from the few flowers and candles that had been offered to it, doesn't attract as much attention as it deserves to!

In *Amante marine*, I pointed to the need for a religious representation and celebration of conception, birth, childhood, adolescence, the female festivals. There are many vestiges of these in Italy (I have cited a few in Northern Italy, since I saw them when attending conferences in those towns) as a result of the Italian people's historical links to the Orient, whose myths patriarchy and Roman law have not always been able to assimilate. But they have been instrumental in turning the meaning of certain realities on their head. Take the numerous Italian paintings of Christ the King crowning the Virgin. It is true that this could take place only after the Last Judgment, which I take to mean after our current systems of representation and judgment have ended. Yet for the scene to be painted, it must be possible to imagine it. It seems to me that this possibility results from a sort of return of a historical repression manifesting itself in an inverted form. Because majesty first belonged to women. Later, they themselves, directly or indirectly, crowned a good many kings in the Orient, in Rome, in France. During entire eras of History, women were queens (as they still are in some cultures . . .) possessing the power of divination. Reading Aeschylus's *Eumenides*, one of the tragedies in the *Oresteia* trilogy, reminds us that women wanted to share oracular power with their boy children. Why did they lose everything along with it: divinity, majesty, identity?

HEAVENLY HORIZONS OR IMPERIALIST DREAMS?

As much as Bachofen provides us with valuable information on gynocratic systems, he doesn't offer a thorough interpretation of the reasons why they passed into patriarchy. I don't think, as he states—along with Hegel, after his fashion—that patriarchy is simply more spiritual than the reigns of women. Bachofen constantly contradicts himself on this, anyway, without resolving his contradictions. In his view, women are more moral, but patriarchy is more spiritual and more celestial. But what do spirituality and heavenliness mean without ethics? A culture feeding off the earth and useful matter, simply to draw apart from them without paying its debts? Perhaps patriarchy has been a necessary stage in History. It cannot mark the end of History if we can see its limitations and are able to interpret them. Today this has become, or has once again become, possible. This task is forced upon us not only out of concern for social justice but also in order to save our natural resources, so that we don't destroy them in the name of a heaven that is simply a construct to overcome the chthonic order. The earth is a resource; we need its minerals, metals, plants, hydrogen, oxygen. It gives us what we need to breathe, to eat, to live. To annihilate the earth is to destroy life, to destroy ourselves. The patriarchal order is based upon worlds of the beyond: worlds of before birth and especially of the afterlife, other planets to be discovered and exploited for survival, etc. It doesn't appreciate the real value of the world we have and draws up its often bankrupt blueprints on the basis of hypothetical worlds. It also believes that everything can be bought. Yet by doing away with female genealogies, along with their respect for the earth and the material world, patriarchal civilizations have also repressed one part of social reality and now have difficulty in rationally envisaging the truth.

TRUTHS AND BELIEFS

One often hears it said that men speak clearly and women don't. Yet male discourse is far from being as clear as people claim. Why? Because male peoples are structured in accordance with civil and religious norms that drastically reduce and transform reality. As a result, the value of words and things has become partly real, partly arbitrary, partly dependent on trust. This makes exchanges between men fundamentally hermetic, as they operate according to rules and conventions that as presently conceived, don't include everyone. The more patriarchal cultures consolidate their power, the more systems of exchange and communication are cut off from individual truth and become the business of specialists and experts alone. This is one of the causes of the difficulties of the modern world. The majority of people no longer know what's true. They give up their right to judge for themselves. They go along with those men or women whom they think know more, whether acceding to supposed capabilities in the social or cultural domain, or, more insidiously, consenting to the manipulation of role models in advertising, sections of the media, art, etc.

Of course, it is impossible for each individual to recreate the whole of History. But I do think that any individual, a woman or a man, can and must recreate her or his personal and collective history. For this to be accomplished, everyone's body and opinions must be respected. Everyone should be able to be aware of her or his obligations, the judge of her or his own decisions. No one ought to believe. This psychic and sociological phenomenon generates dangerous artificial powers. Belief destroys identity and responsibility and goes against what experience teaches. It often further reinforces those historical gaps or oversights, whether these are exercised in the economy of discourses or in the systems of images that go with them.

April 1987

3

WOMEN'S DISCOURSE AND MEN'S DISCOURSE

How can the indicators of the sexed character of discourse be analyzed? In order to carry out such a study, I first collected material in French. I made tapes of men and women in daily situations and in a therapy context. With the help of several female and male colleagues I also asked groups of men and women to participate in short linguistic tests along the following lines: "Make a simple sentence using one of the given prompt words: single, marriage, sexuality, child, etc." or "Make a simple sentence using one of the following word groups: boredom—him/her—speak; dress—oneself— see; house—mother; house—table; etc." or "Give the opposite, the synonym, or the definition of given words of various grammatical categories and varying degrees of ambiguity."

I have begun to sort through and interpret the responses we obtained. I can already affirm that similar characteristics can be found in all the women's statements, on the one hand, and in all the men's, on the other. In this respect, it's fair to say that their discourses are sexed. Indicators of belonging to a particular sex appeared to be more significant than variables of context, more important than changing the interlocutor as a contextual factor of the experimental situation.

What can we make of this? The process of drawing conclusions from this sort of work has to be lengthy because of the significance of the issues at stake and the strong feelings they arouse, whether consciously or unconsciously. What I will do then is outline a few questions that this research—still in progress, particularly internationally[1]—has enabled me to formulate or reformulate with the support of research evidence.

THE EFFECTS OF SOCIETY OR OF LANGUAGE?

Are the differences between men's and women's statements the effects of society or of language? I think this division should be denied. Language is a product of the sedimentations of languages of former eras. It conveys their methods of social communication. It's neither universal, nor neutral, nor intangible. There are no universal linguistic structures in the brain of the speaking subject; rather, every era has its specific needs, creates its own ideals, and imposes them as such. Some are more historically durable than others: sexual ideals are a good example here. These ideals have gradually imposed their norms on our language. Hence, in French:

[1] Cf. *Sexes et Genres à Travers les Langues* (Paris: Grasset, 1990): A collection of research into the English, French, and Italian languages, edited by Luce Irigaray.

---

1. The masculine is always dominant in syntax: *ils sont mariés* (they are married), *ils s'aiment* (they love each other), *ils sont beaux* (they are beautiful), etc. This grammatical mark, which erases the feminine,[2] has an impact on the way subjectivity is experienced and the way it is expressed in and by discourse.

2. The neuter or impersonal is expressed by the same pronoun or in the same form as the masculine: *il tonne* (it's thundering), *il neige* (it's snowing), *il faut* (it's necessary), not *elle tonne, elle neige, elle faut*. Even if, in the history of the language, certain objects were qualified as neuter (in Greek and Latin, for example), natural phenomena and necessity were designated as being sexed. Likewise, the *il faut* or *il est nécessaire* of the Greek philosophers, or their descendants, hides a sexual necessity related both to human and to divine destiny. The origin of necessity is not neutral. Only later did it become so, particularly through subjection to the order of Roman law. But then laws were decreed solely by men. *Il faut* signifies an obligation or an order set up by one sexed subject alone. It only appears to be neutral, and once again, in French at least, it's expressed in the same way as the masculine.

Man seems to have wanted, directly or indirectly, to give the universe his own gender as he has wanted to give his own name to his children, his wife, his possessions. This has

---

[2] In French the plural always takes the masculine form (*ils*) when this plural is comprised of both masculine and feminine substantives; only when the plural is comprised exclusively of feminine substantives does it take the feminine form (*elles*). (Tr.)

a significant bearing upon the sexes'[3] relationships to the world, to things, to objects. In fact, anything believed to have value belongs to men and is marked by their gender. Apart from possessions in the strict sense that man attributes to himself, he gives his own gender to God, to the sun, and also, in the guise of the neuter, to the laws of the cosmos and of the social or individual order. He doesn't even question the genealogy of this attribution.

In French (along with other Romance languages), the feminine remains secondary syntactically, not even a norm, and nouns marked by the feminine are not those considered to designate the greater value. In French, the moon is feminine, as are the stars, yet neither are generally thought of as sources of life. As for the earth, it is carved up into parcels that men share among themselves, destroying or masking the unity of the feminine.[4]

How could discourse not be sexed when language is? It is sexed in some of its most fundamental rules, in the division of words into gender in a way not unrelated to sexual connotations or qualities, just as the lexicon is sexed, too. Differences between men's and women's discourses are thus the effects of language and society, society and language. You

---

[3] Irigaray at this point explains that she often uses the word *sexe* (sex)—often used to refer to the sexual organs in French—instead of *genre* (gender) in order to avoid the traditional connotations associated with the latter, which may refer to grammatical gender, a style of discourse, or the ostensibly universal *genre humain* (humankind); she also uses it to make reference to the subject of enunciation rather than to the subject of the statement (l'*énoncé*). (Tr.)

[4] "*L'unité du genre feminin.*" Given that the earth (*la terre*) is feminine, this sentence plays on the ambiguities of the word *genre* to suggest the unity of both the feminine grammatical gender and the global female kind. (Tr.)

can't change one without changing the other. Yet while it's impossible to radically separate one from the other, we can shift the emphasis of cultural transformation from one to the other, above all we must not wait, passively, for language to progress. Issues of discourse and of language can be deliberately used to attain greater cultural maturity, more social justice. It's the lack of consideration given to the importance of this dimension of culture that gives the technological empire so much power as a neutral force, that reinforces sectarian setbacks, present-day social and cultural disintegration, the various monocratic imperialisms, etc.

SEXUAL LIBERATION IMPLIES LINGUISTIC TRANSFORMATIONS

It must be emphasized, too, that sexual liberation cannot be achieved without changing the laws of language that relate to gender. Subjective liberation requires language free from rules that constrain sexual difference or cancel it out (though if this were at all possible, it would be by magic). The points to examine and modify can vary from one language to another. One mustn't forget this. But I know of no current language that has thought out its status as a tool of sharing and exchange between two parties belonging to the world of different sexes. Individual decision-making and collective good will can only be thwarted in their projects for sexual liberation and social justice if they don't consider the theoretical and practical impact of the sexed marks and rules of language, with a view to modifying this instrument of culture.

The statements analyzed show a significant difference between men and women in terms of sexual interrelation. Women sexualize their discourse. Just as they often attribute their concrete qualities to things and to places, they address themselves to sexed interlocutors. Men don't do this but remain among themselves, between they (ils), or between I-he/they (je-il(s)), which is equivalent to making a non-conscious sexual choice.

Should women give up sexualizing their partner of enunciation? I hope they don't. Sex is an important dimension of culture, but we have to redress the balance of power in relationships between the sexes in language, society, culture. It would be better if women, without ceasing to put sexual difference into words, were more able to situate themselves as I, I-she / they (je-elle[s]), to represent themselves as subjects, and to talk to other women. That requires a development in subjectivity and a transformation of the rules of language. To date, women have had to remain among themselves not only in order for a plural to be feminine—elles s'aiment (they love each other), elles sont belles (they are beautiful)—but also for a relationship to the subjectively female world to be possible.[5] This linguistic necessity lays the basis for certain sorts of liberation movements. The human world cannot, however, be split between men and women without any point of contact. Unless they're silent? But silence itself is related to the discourse being spoken. Single-sex strategies are essential when it comes explicitly to matters of content in discourse, but even more so in the case of the forms and laws of language. The aim must be to alter these in order to be effective in systems of exchange, including among women.

What the analysis of the various research material has made clear is that the you (tu) of women's discourse refers to a woman in the psychoanalytic transfer, though admittedly this

[5] See footnote above, p. 25 (Tr).

took place with a woman as the support. Yet in the experimental statements, the partner of enunciation is designated as *he/they* (*il(s)*), even when those conducting the experiment are women. What can we make of this change from *you* (*tu*) as the medium? Is it a cultural erasure? Is it the imposition of a pseudo-neutrality, tellingly reintroducing a masculine *he* (*il*) in place of a feminine *you* (*tu*)? Both sexes make this gender substitution. Seen in terms of a subject's history, it leads to the erasure of the relationship with the first *you* (*tu*), the mother. As a result the passage from *you-she-I* (*tu-elle-je*) is missing for women, a loss of sexual identity in the relation to herself and to her gender, especially genealogically. For men, the originally maternal-feminine *you* (*tu*) is lost in favor of *he*. It's the transition from *you-she-you* (*tu-elle-tu*) that language lacks. This corresponds to the syntactical economy of the discourses analyzed and to findings concerning our linguistic order, in which the maternal *you* (*tu*) and the female *I* (*je*) are wiped out. This order is not arbitrary but is impelled by laws that have escaped the attention of linguists.

TWO DIFFERENT WORLDS

Most of the time, in *men's discourse*, the world is designated as inanimate abstractions integral to the subject's world. Reality appears as an always already cultural reality, linked to the individual and collective history of the masculine subject. It's always a matter of a secondary nature, cut off from its corporeal roots, its cosmic environment, its relation to life. This relation is only ever mentioned to be denied, and is perpetually passing into uncultured behavior. The forms may change, but the blind immediacy of the behavior stays the same. The male subject's relations to his body, to what it has given him, to nature, to the bodies of others, including those of his sexual partners, are yet to be developed. In the meantime, the realities of which his discourse speaks are artificial, mediated to such an extent by one subject and one culture that it's not really possible to share them. Yet that's what language is for. Furthermore, these realities are so far distanced from life that they become deadly, as Freud predicted when he spoke of the cultural primacy of death drives.

Women's discourse designates men as subjects—except in the psychoanalytic transfer—and the world as concrete inanimate objects belonging to the universe of the other. Women thus maintain a relationship to the real environment but they don't subjectivize it as their own. They remain the locus for the experience of concrete reality, but they leave the matter of its structuration to the other. It's true that language doesn't give them the means to do otherwise; at least, it hasn't for centuries. The connotations of women's discourse are primarily expressed in privileged ways—through adjectives, for example—and not in the predicate that is currently produced. Linguistically, that might mean that the language they use at present corresponds to an altered version of a discourse they used in former times (and/or that in this they resist the later characteristics of male discourse). Other indications— the elisions of *I* and *she*, all the strategies for erasing the feminine as the subject of discourse, the issue of negative transformation—can be interpreted in this way. This will form the basis of my future research on the sex and gender of the subject in discourse and language.

The world changes. Nowadays, its development seems to threaten life and the creation of values. Those values remaining are often subject to the reign of money. The means for communication that operate in societies completely in the hands of men might well prevent the emergence of or destroy other means of communication that relate more closely to life, to its concrete properties. The sexed dimension is one of the most important, not only for reproduction but also for culture and the preservation of life. The issue, then, is one of whether our civilizations are still prepared to consider sex as pathological, a flaw, a residue of animality, or if they are finally mature enough to give it its human cultural status. It's a transformation that will come through the development of the sexed dimension of language and every single means of exchange.

June 1987

4

ON THE MATERNAL ORDER

It would seem we are generally subject to two behavioral models: the Darwinian model and the Pavlovian model.

1. As far as life is concerned, we are said to be always struggling against the external environment, on the one hand, and with other living beings, on the other. Only by being stronger than these two adversaries are we able to stay alive.
2. At the level of culture, it seems we are brought up (whether consciously or not) to be trained in repetition, to adapt to a society's systems, and educated to do like, to be like, without any decisive innovations or discoveries of our own.

Can we get away from these two great structures and their variants? Can we free ourselves from competitive combat at the level of existence? From almost fatal repetition at the cultural level? Of the interrelation of the two in social (dis)organizations? Do the issues of sexual identity, and particularly of female identity, as yet unresolved, give us the means to do so? I would say they do. If this doesn't seem at all obvious, then I would interpret that as a further indication of the influence of Darwinism and Pavlovism. We are struggling against all forms of others to be able to live, and we are still subject to conditioned social rules that we confuse with freedom: hence a single sex or gender and not two, the (patriarchal) culture we are familiar with and no other. It seems to me, though, that given the economy of sexual difference, as well as that of the laws of the universe, these great models have to face their limitations.

The placental relation represents one of these openings with regard to determinism, to vital or cultural closure, an opening which stems from female corporeal identity. Hélène Rouch, a biology teacher at the *Lycée Colbert* in Paris, has studied the singularity of the relations between mother and child in *utero*. These relations, which the patriarchal imagination often presents (for example, in psychoanalysis) as in a state of fusion, are in fact strangely organized and respectful of the life of both.

BELONGING TO NEITHER ONE NOR THE OTHER

Luce Irigaray: *Hélène, can you explain the mediating role the placenta plays during interuterine life?*

Hélène Rouch: Firstly, I'll just remind us what the placenta is: it's a tissue, formed by the embryo, which, while being closely imbricated with the uterine mucosa remains separate from it. This has to be reiterated, because there's a commonly held view that the placenta is a mixed formation, half-maternal, half-fetal. However, although the placenta is a formation of the embryo, it behaves like an organ that is practically independent of it. It plays a mediating role on two levels. On the one hand, it's the mediating space between mother and fetus, which means that there's never a fusion of maternal and embryonic tissues. On the other hand, it constitutes a system regulating exchanges between the two organisms, not merely quantitatively regulating the exchanges (nutritious substances from mother to fetus, waste matter in the other direction), but also modifying the maternal metabolism: transforming, storing, and redistributing maternal substances for both her own and the fetus' benefit. It thus establishes a relationship between mother and fetus, enabling the latter to grow without exhausting the mother in the process, and yet not simply being a means for obtaining nutritious substances.

As far as hormones are concerned, the placental role is just as interesting. For an initial period it takes over from the maternal hypothalamus to maintain ovarian secretions needed during gestation. Then later it takes over from the ovary itself by producing steroids which go to both mother and fetus. In addition, it seems to have an auto-control system enabling it to regulate its own hormonal secretions. So what we have here is an organ that, although anatomically dependent upon the embryo, secretes maternal hormones that are essential during gestation when the maternal organism finds itself unable to continue its usual ovarian function owing to the state of pregnancy.

This relative autonomy of the placenta, its regulatory functions ensuring the growth of the one in the body of the other, cannot be reduced either to a mechanism of fusion (an ineffable mixture of the bodies or blood of mother and fetus), or, conversely, to one of aggression (the fetus as foreign body devouring from the inside, a vampire in the maternal body). These descriptions are of imaginary reality and appear quite poor indeed—and obviously extremely culturally determined—in comparison to the complexity of biological reality.

PEACEFUL COEXISTENCE

L. I.: *Can you explain the difference between problems with transplants, with immunity, and what's peculiar to the placental economy concerning phenomena of rejection of the other?*

H. R.: You could say that pregnancy constitutes a successful transplant. We have great difficulty successfully transplanting an organ from one individual to another, yet here it's done naturally. With a transplant, the problem is that the receiving organism recognizes the transplanted organ as foreign and so activates immune mechanisms aimed at rejecting this foreign body. The recognition is carried out by a system of markers, or antigens, specific to each individual and for this reason called self-antigens. In organ transplants, this problem is resolved either by choosing a donor who is genetically as close as possible to the receiver (the ideal transplant being between identical twins), or by diminishing activity leading to the rejection of the organ by means of immunodepressors, which obviously renders the receiver extremely vulnerable to other infections.

The embryo is half-foreign to the maternal organism. Indeed, half of its antigens are paternal in origin. Because of these, the mother should activate her defense mechanisms to reject this other to her self. The placenta, which is also this

———

other, prevents this mechanism from being activated. In a complex manner, it will block or at the very least greatly minimize maternal activity leading to rejection, but only locally, around the uterus, and moreover in such a way that the mother keeps her defensive capacities against potential infection.

L. I.: *Can you briefly explain the immune paradox and the question of the same and the other in relation to the acceptability or rejection of the embryo as foreign body?*

H. R.: It's more than a paradox. It's a sort of negotiation between the mother's self and the other that is the embryo. In fact, placental mechanisms designed to block maternal immune reactions are only put into operation if there has been a recognition, by the maternal organism, of foreign antigens. Thus, the placenta isn't some sort of automatic protection system, which would suppress all the mother's reaction by preventing it from recognizing the embryo-fetus as other. On the contrary, there has to be a recognition of the other, of the non-self, by the mother, and therefore an initial reaction from her, in order for placental factors to be produced. The difference between the "self" and other is, so to speak, continuously negotiated. It's as if the mother always knew that the embryo (and thus the placenta) was other, and that she lets the placenta know this, which then produces the factors enabling the maternal organism to accept it as other. These tolerance mechanisms are to be distinguished both from the case of transplants—in which the transplanted organ, recognized as other, immediately and irrevocably activates an immune reaction, causing rejection by the receiver—and from that of particular cancerous tumors

───────

35

which, not recognized as others, proliferate in the defenseless organism.

CULTURAL AMNESIA

L. I.: *The placental economy is therefore an organized economy, one not in a state of fusion, which respects the one and the other. Unfortunately, our cultures, split off from the natural order—and the scientific methods used to get back to it more often than not accentuate that distance—neglect or fail to recognize the almost ethical character of the fetal relation. In the article you wrote for the issue of* Langages *on* Le sexe linguistique[1] *you give several indications as to the consequences of the ignorance of the placental economy on the male cultural imaginary, in particular regarding the relationship to the so-called mother tongue. Could you summarize that part of your work here?*

H. R.: First of all, I'll digress to look at psychoanalysis, which justifies the imaginary fusion between a child and its mother by the undeveloped state of the child at birth and by its absolute need of the other, its mother. It's this fusion, implicitly presented as an extension of the organic fusion during pregnancy, which, it would seem, simply has to be broken in order for the child to be constituted as a subject. The rupture of this fusion by a third term—whether it's called the father, law, Name of the Father, or something else— should facilitate entry into the symbolic and access to language. This third term supposedly avoids the fusion that would lead into the chaos of psychosis, and is said to guarantee order. But surely all that's needed is to reiterate and mark, on another level, a differentiation that already exists during

---

[1] "Le placenta comme tiers," *op. cit.*

---

pregnancy thanks to the placenta and at the moment of birth, as a result of the exit from the uterine cavity? It seems to me that the differentiation between the mother's self and the other of the child, and vice versa, is in place well before it's given meaning in and by language, and the forms it takes don't necessarily accord with those our cultural imaginary relays: loss of paradise, traumatizing expulsion or exclusion, etc. I'm not accusing these forms of the imaginary of being wrong, but of being the only ways of theorizing what exists before language. It makes one wonder about this remarkable blindness to the processes of pregnancy, and especially to the particular role of the placenta, even though nowadays they're quite familiar.

In my study I took Michel Serres's book *The Parasite* as an example of this blindness; I thought it paradigmatic of male relationships with the mother tongue. In this book, Serres on the one hand rails against man, the parasite of fauna and flora, who takes all and gives nothing; on the other hand, he vaunts the delights of his relations with the mother tongue, which gives him everything and yet which he still finds "intact and virginal" after he (and several friends) have endlessly feasted with her. Therefore man never gives anything, but all the same he speaks, consumes a language that is inexhaustible and never stops being miraculously renewed. Hence for Serres the incarnation of Christ is a miracle, as he is the only human who gives himself "to be eaten" in communion. But who does offer their body as food if not a pregnant woman? Except she's not to be found "virginal" nor "intact" at the end of her pregnancy. Serres knows this, because he calls the fetus a parasite. Yet instead of acknowledging every human being's debt, he would rather forget and speak: to speak of and with a language that has the maternal body's gifts of generosity, abundance, and plenitude, but to which nothing is owed. The materiality of the relationship to this maternal body having disappeared, language remains an inexhaustible "womb" for the use that's made of her.

THE PROFIT OF NEGLECT

L. I.: *What's your position on the commercial use of the placenta?*

H. R.: Doctors say placentas are thrown in the dustbin. But it's common knowledge that they are sold commercially, legally or illegally, to both public and private research laboratories and institutes, because they provide excellent material for medical and scientific research, and for the cosmetics industry. The two domains aren't separate, even if what's profited by them is different. There's nothing wrong in wanting to study the properties of the placenta and in using its therapeutic virtues. What is scandalous, however, is the enormous profit cosmetic industries gain from their use.

The placenta is the child's organ that owes its development to the mother's body. If she isn't the owner of it as such, she could be asked to whom or for what she would like to make a gift of it. That would be a mark, symbolically at least, of the gift she has given to the child and the debt, inestimable in our patriarchal commercial system, of the child in return.

July 1987

5

THE CULTURE
OF DIFFERENCE

One of the distinctive features of the female body is its toleration of the other's growth within itself without incurring illness or death for either one of the living organisms. Unfortunately, culture has practically inverted the meaning of this economy of respect for the other. It has blindly venerated the mother-son relationship to the point of religious fetishism, but has given no interpretation to the model of tolerance of the other within and with a self that this relationship manifests. A woman's body in fact gives equal opportunities of life to the boys and to the girls conceived in it through the coming together of male and female chromosomes.

The between-men culture works in the opposite sense. The way it is structured excludes what the other sex brings to its society. Whereas the female body engenders with respect for difference, the patriarchal social body constructs itself hierarchically, excluding difference. Woman-as-other has to remain the natural substratum in this social construction, a substratum whose importance remains unclear in its relational signification. Clearly, the cult of the mother-son relationship demonstrates female tolerance. Yet, to date, girls are also engendered by male semen. They are not produced partheno-genetically by their mother, even if the outcome of the chromosomal encounter is the birth of a child who resembles her.

Our civilizations, therefore, are lacking in two respects; they present us with two repressions, two injustices or anomalies:

1. women, who have given life and growth to the other within themselves, are excluded from the order of the same which men alone set up
2. the girl child, although conceived by a man and a woman, doesn't enter society as the father's child with the same status as that accorded the son. She remains outside culture, kept as a natural body good only for procreation.

The difficulties women have in gaining recognition for their social and political rights are rooted in this insufficiently thought out relation between biology and culture. At present, to deny all explanations of a biological kind—because bio-logy has paradoxically been used to exploit women—is to deny the key to interpreting this exploitation. It also comes down to remaining within the cultural naïveté that dates back to when the men-gods established their reign: only that which mani-fests itself in the form of a man is the divine child of the father, only that showing an immediate resemblance to the father may be legitimized as a valued son. The deformed or the atypical are to be hidden in shame. And as for women, they have to reside in darkness, behind veils, indoors; they are stripped of their identity insofar as they are a non-manifestation of forms corresponding to male-sexed chromosomes.

In order to obtain a subjective status equivalent to that of men, women must therefore gain recognition for their difference. They must affirm themselves as valid subjects, daughters of a mother and a father, respecting the other within themselves and demanding that same respect from society.

Yet the whole framework of their identity has to be constructed, or reconstructed. I'd like to suggest a few simple examples of the way identity relations between mothers and daughters might be improved, as this is the least cultured space of our societies. Indeed, such relations are subject to a double exclusion from patriarchal cultures because the woman is rejected from them as woman subject, and the daughter is not given equal recognition as girl subject. The values dominating our civilizations are those that show clearly they belong to the male gender.

How can we get out of this vicious circle of the patriarchal phallocratic order? How are we to give girls the possibility of spirit or soul? We can do it through subjective relations between mothers and daughters. The following, then, are a few practical suggestions for the development of mother-daughter relationships.

1. Learn once again to respect life and nourishment. Which means regaining respect for the mother and nature. We often forget that not all debts can be paid by money alone and that not all nourishment can be bought. This is a point that obviously concerns boy children, too, but it's vital for the rediscovery of a female identity.
2. In all homes and all public places, attractive images (not involving advertising) of the mother-daughter couple

should be displayed. It's very damaging for girls always to be faced with representations of mother and son, especially in the religious dimension. I'd suggest to all Christian women, for example, that they place an image depicting Mary and her mother Anne in their living room, in their daughters' rooms, and in their own room. There are sculptures and easily reproducible paintings of them available. I'd also advise them to display photographs of themselves with their daughter(s), or maybe with their mother. They could also have photographs of the triangle: mother, father, daughter. The point of these representations is to give girls a valid representation of their genealogy, an essential condition for the constitution of their identity.

3. I suggest mothers create opportunities to use the feminine plural with their daughter(s). They could also invent words and expressions to designate realities they feel and share but for which they lack language.

4. It's also important for mothers and daughters to find or make objects they can exchange between themselves so that they can be defined as female I↔you (je↔tu). I say "exchangeable" since objects that may be shared, divided, and consumed together can maintain unity. Normally, women only exchange remarks to do with children, food, or perhaps their appearance and sexual exploits. These are not exchangeable objects. Yet to speak well of oneself and others, it helps to be able to communicate about the realities of the world, to be able to exchange something.

5. It would be helpful if, from an early age, mothers taught daughters respect for the non-hierarchical difference of the sexes: *he* means *he*, *she* means *she*. *He* and *she* cannot be reduced to complementary functions but correspond to different identities. Women and men, mothers and fathers,

girls and boys have different forms and qualities. They can't be identified solely through actions or roles alone.

6. To establish and maintain relations with oneself and with the other, space is essential. Often women are confined to the inner spaces of their womb or their sex insofar as they serve procreation and male desire. It's important for them to have their own outer space, enabling them to go from the inside to the outside of themselves, to experience themselves as autonomous and free subjects. How can the creation of this space between mothers and daughters be given a chance? The following are a few suggestions:

(a) As often as possible, substitute human value for artificial value.

(b) Avoid being exiled from natural and cosmic space.

(c) Play with mirror phenomena, with symmetrical and asymmetrical phenomena (particularly right-left) to minimize the chances of being projected into or devoured by the other, and of indifferentiation with the other: whether the mother, the father, future lover, etc.

(d) Learn not always to follow the same path, which doesn't mean to dissipate your energies, but rather to know how to circulate from outside to inside, from inside to outside yourself.

(e) Between mother and daughter, interpose small handmade objects to make up for the losses of spatial identity, for intrusions into personal space.

(f) Don't restrict yourself to describing, reproducing, and repeating what exists, but know how to invent or imagine what hasn't yet taken place.

(g) In verbal exchanges, create sentences in which I-woman (*je-femme*) talks to you-woman (*tu-femme*), particularly of yourself or of a third woman. The fact that this sort of language barely exists greatly restricts women's space for subjective freedom. It's possible to start to create it with everyday language. Mothers and daughters could do it in affective and educational games. In concrete terms, that means that the mother-woman should speak to the daughter-woman, use feminine grammatical forms, talk about things that concern the two of them, talk about herself and ask her daughter to do the same, bring up her genealogy, especially the relation to her own mother, tell her daughter about women currently involved in public life, or Historical or mythological women, ask her daughter to tell her about her girlfriends, and so on. When girls start school, the discourse they learn is that of he/they (*il(s)*), or the between-men culture (*l'entre-il(s)*). Even if coeducational schools do have some advantages, in this respect they are not particularly favorable to the development of girls' identity as long as linguistic rules (grammatical, semantic, lexicological) don't progress.

Today, only a mother can see to it that her daughter, her daughters, form(s) a girl's identity. Daughters that we are, more aware of the issues concerning our liberation, we can also educate our mothers and educate each other among ourselves. I think this is essential for the social and cultural changes we need.

September 1987

6

WRITING AS A WOMAN

Alice Jardine: *What does it mean to you to write at the end of the twentieth century?* [1]

Luce Irigaray: It means several things; I'll list those I can think of right now:

1. I live at the end of the twentieth century and I am of an age to write.
2. I earn my living by writing. I am not a woman supported by a man or men; I have to meet my own material needs. I do scientific research and my job is to work on particular issues and to pass on the results of my work.
3. One means of communicating thought, in the late

---

[1] This interview was carried out by Alice Jardine and Anne Menke of Harvard University. It is part of a study of women's writing.

---

twentieth century, is by alphabetical writing. Thus, I use it to communicate even if I think this method is limiting to what I have to say, especially as a woman.

4. Writing enables me to transmit my thought to many people whom I don't know, who don't speak the same language as I do, don't live at the same time as I do. In this respect, writing means creating a corpus and a code of meaning which can be stored and circulated, and which is likely to go down in History. Taking the form(s) and content(s) of my discourse, my use of writing in this latter part of the twentieth century signifies an attempt to create a new cultural era: that of sexual difference. It seems to me that this is a necessary task at this moment in History in terms of the past, the present, and the future.

5. To some extent I was prevented from expressing myself orally when my book *Speculum* was published. I had a university post and I was relieved of it. Fortunately, I wasn't removed from my research post at the National Center for Scientific Research. Fortunately, too, I write, and Editions de Minuit have continued to publish my work. Writing can therefore be a means of expressing yourself and of communicating in certain circumstances when you are denied the right to speak.

6. Being denied the right to speak can have several meanings and take several forms. It can be a conscious effort to ban someone from institutions, or to banish him or her from the *polis*. Such an action can mean, if only in part: I don't understand what you're doing so I reject it, we reject it. In this case, writing allows your thought to be put on hold, to be available to those women and men who sooner or later will be able to understand it. This applies to some

---

areas of knowledge more than others, and for various reasons the discourse seeking to establish a new sexed culture is one of them.

A. J.: *Writing as a woman: is this valid and does it enter into your practice as a writer?*

L. I.:   I am a woman. I write with who I am. Why wouldn't that be valid, unless out of contempt for the value of women or from a denial of a culture in which the sexual is a significant subjective and objective dimension? But how could I on the one hand be a woman, and on the other, a writer? Only those who are still in a state of verbal automatism or who mimic already existing meaning can maintain such a scission or split between she who is a woman and she who writes. The whole of my body is sexuate. My sexuality isn't restricted to my sex and to the sexual act (in the narrow sense). I think the effects of repression and especially the lack of sexual culture—civil and religious—are still so powerful that they enable such strange statements to be upheld as "I am a woman" and "I do not write as a woman." In these protestations there's also a secret allegiance to the between-men cultures. Indeed, alphabetical writing is linked historically to the civil and religious codification of patriarchal powers. Not to contribute to making language and its writings sexed is to perpetuate the pseudo-neutrality of those laws and traditions that privilege masculine genealogies and their codes of logic.

A. J.: *Many women writing today find themselves for the first time historically within institutions, such as universities or psychoanalysis. In your view, will this new place for women help get them into the twentieth-century canon,* and will that be at the very heart of this corpus or will they (still) be kept to the footnotes?

L. I.:   At the present time, there aren't that many women working in institutions. Those that do are often restricted in how far they can go in their career. Very few women reach the highest posts and they pay very dearly for it, in one way or another. That this is true is shown by the debates concerning names for occupations.

However, in order to write things that will be inscribed into and remain in the memory of the twentieth century, just being in an institution isn't enough. It sometimes enables thought to be spread rapidly, but that gives no indication of what its historical impact will be. It's quite possible that many of the women who are allowed into institutions talk about a culture that has already passed and not about what will remain as a trace of the elaboration of the present and the future.

Where will this civilization, which is in the course of construction, be expressed? Not just in writing, that's for sure! However, taking the written corpus alone, the footnotes are often the least accessible place for women. Because in these a name has to be cited, as well as the title of the book or article, and precise references to a text have to be given; at least that's what I understand. Some women's work has already entered into the body of books, but it's often been assimilated without a precise indication of who produced it. Culture has taught us to consume the mother's body—natural and spiritual—without being indebted and, as far as the world of men is concerned, to mark this appropriation with their name. Your question seems to suggest that this cannot change. Women's words are to remain in the main body or in the notes of a text they have neither written nor signed by their name. Unless the way your question has been put or translated is incorrect?

What's most difficult to understand in History are the different contributions men and women make to civilization. A sign of the reality and recognition of this would be the publication of books signed by women that contribute to the elaboration of culture in a manner irreplaceably theirs, not that of men. Another indication of a transformation in the order of symbolic exchanges would be a proliferation of texts showing a real dialogue between women and men.

A. J.: Nowadays we are witnessing the production of literary, philosophical, and psychoanalytical theory by women that is recognized as being significant, and at the same time, a new fluidity between the boundaries of disciplines and between styles of writing. Will these two parallel movements lead to women merely being welcomed alongside nun or to the definitive blurring of the distinctions between categories?

L. I.: There is not a great amount of fluidity between disciplines and styles of writing these days. The many fields of knowledge and techniques have made the boundaries between forms of knowledge more watertight now than they were in the past. In previous centuries, there was a dialogue between philosophers and scientists. Nowadays, they are often complete strangers to each other because their languages don't enable them to communicate with one another.

Are there new areas of exchange between disciplines such as philosophy, psychoanalysis, and literature? This is a complex question. There are attempts to pass from one field to another but they are not always successful because they lack the necessary scope. What we are witnessing is a modification in the use of language by certain philosophers who are

---

returning to their cultural origins. Thus, Nietzsche, Heidegger, and Hegel before them question their Greek foundations, their religious foundations, Derrida his relationship to the books of the Old Testament. For them this move goes along with using a style which is close to that of tragedy, poetry, the Platonic dialogues, mythical expression, religious acts and parables. This return is a return to the moment when male identity was constituted as patriarchal and phallocratic. Is it women's emergence from the home and silence that has forced men to ask themselves a few questions? All the latter philosophers— except Heidegger—are explicitly interested in female identity, sometimes in their own identity as feminine or women. Will this lead to the blurring of the distinctions between categories? Which ones? In the name of what? Or whom? Why? I think what you call categories are areas of knowledge and not the logical categories of discourse and of truth. The establishment of new logical forms or rules has to be accompanied by a new subjective identity, new rules for determining signification. Which is also a prerequisite for women to be able to situate themselves in cultural production alongside and with men. In turning back toward the moment when they seized sociocultural power(s), are men looking for a way to divest themselves of those powers? I hope so. This would imply that they are inviting women to share in the definition and exercise of truth with them. Writing differently has not, as yet, done much to change the sex of political leaders nor their civil and religious discourses.

Is it just a matter of patience? Should we be patient faced with decisions made on our behalf and in our name? Of course, as far as I'm concerned, there's no question of us turning to violence, but we should investigate ways of giving an identity to the sciences, to religions, and to political policies and of situating ourselves in relation to them as subjects in our own right. Literature is fine. But how can we bring the world of men to govern peoples poetically when what they are interested in above all is money, competition for power, and so on? And how can we govern the world as women if we have not defined our identity, the rules concerning our genealogical relationships, our social, linguistic, and cultural order? Psychoanalysis can be a great help to us in this task if we know how to use it in a way suited to our spiritual and corporeal needs and desires. It can help us to draw away from patriarchal culture, provided we don't allow ourselves to be defined by nor attracted to the male genealogical world's theories and problems.

A. J.:   *Given the problematic and the politics of the categories of the canon, and given the issues we've touched on here, will your work find a place in the twentieth-century canon, and how will it be presented within it? In your view, what might the contents of this canon be?*

L. I.:   In this question I detect a wish to anticipate and define the future rather than to work now to construct it. Being concerned for the future in the present is certainly not equivalent to programming it in advance but rather to trying to make it exist. That said, from the moment a dozen of your essays have been in bookstores and public and private libraries for several years and they have been translated into several languages, they have a chance of figuring in the twentieth-century canon. Unless a cataclysm occurs and does away with any possibility of such a canon?

Perhaps this cataclysm is to be found in what you intend by the word *canon*. Actually, I don't see what enables you to talk about the "problematic and politics of the categories of the

———

51

canon." What you suggest seems to presuppose that all that is decided as of now, that there will only be the past in the future, that the female and male readers living beyond the twentieth century will have no part in deciding what will define the twentieth-century canon. You also appear to assert that there will only be *one* canon and it will have only *one* content. I'm surprised by that. If there's only one, it would have to be rigorously programmed by the forms of its expression; it would represent an immutable framework of language.

You seem to ignore the fact that there are several languages and that they evolve. Take the question of gender, for example, which not all languages treat the same way. With your hypothesis we come back to the problem of knowing which language will win out over the others. In that there is very much a cataclysmic horizon to which I couldn't subscribe, no more than I could adhere to the belief that there are universals programming meaning, eternally and globally, for all men and for all women. That being said, I could give the following response to your question: will the future emphasize the subject or the object? communication and exchanges of meaning or the possession of material goods? To these alternatives, which in part correspond to the different expression of gender in particular Romance and Germanic languages, my response is that I wouldn't wish ancient cultural traditions to be abolished by civilizations that are less developed in terms of subjectivity. I would like the culture of the subject to which I belong, notably owing to my language, to progress toward a culture of the sexed subject and not toward a thoughtless destruction of subjectivity. Looked at in these terms, I very much hope to figure in the cultural memory of the twentieth century and to contribute to the transformations in the forms and contents of discourse. For me this wish goes hand in hand with a hope for a future that is *more* rather than *less* cultured than the past or present, a future in which symbolic exchanges will be more free, more just, and more developed than at present, including in the religious dimension which the word "canon" evokes.

A. J.:   *Are you as convinced as you were in 1974, when* Speculum *was published, that the introduction of the female body into the male corpus is an essential strategy?*

L. I.:   It makes me wonder how *Speculum* was translated in America for me to hear such misunderstandings of this book. Of course, it is a difficult book, as it defines a new horizon of thought. *Speculum* is also extremely difficult to translate given that the writing plays on the synonymy or homonymy of French words and their syntactic and semantic ambiguities. In this sense it's untranslatable. But, apart from the translation, I think there are other reasons for these misunderstandings. I suspect that one of these is the reduction of fact to rumor or opinion on the part of those who haven't actually read the text.

Thus, *Speculum* cannot suggest getting the "female body" to enter into the male corpus, as the female body has always figured in the male corpus—not always in philosophy, it's true, although it can be found there as well. I'm obviously aware of that. *Speculum* criticizes the exclusive right of the use(s), exchange(s), representation(s) of one sex by the other. This critique is accompanied by the beginnings of a woman's phenomenological elaboration of the auto-affection and auto-representation of her body: Luce Irigaray, signatory to the book. What this implies is that the female body is not to remain the object of men's discourse or their various arts but that it become the object of a female subjectivity experiencing

53

and identifying itself. Such research attempts to suggest to women a morpho-logic that is appropriate to their bodies. It's aimed at the male subject, too, inviting him to redefine himself as a body with a view to exchanges between sexed subjects.

Working for this social and cultural transformation remains the basis for my work, the emphasis shifting from one sector of culture to another, with the intention of rethinking its constitution.

Might there be, perhaps, in your question, a note of surprise at the fact that the sexed body could enter into the definition of subjectivity and culture? I think this area of research constitutes one of the tasks of our time, following particularly from the discovery of the unconscious and the various human liberation movements.

September 1987

7

"I WON'T GET AIDS"[1]

Recently I heard a twenty-five-year-old man, a philosophy student, intelligent, politicized, etc., state that AIDS would contribute to the creation of a new sexual ethics. His argument was that, faced with having to avoid certain erogenous zones, sexual partners, especially men, would find themselves forced to make their desires more refined and sophisticated. He gave some examples of couples he knew quite well.

I don't doubt this man's sincerity. What's more, I have already heard this sort of argument given during some television programs about AIDS. These remarks seem tragicomic to me—that a so-called developed civilization like ours should need catastrophies to improve love-making. Such a conception of sexual ethics reeks of the most repressive and ideological

---

[1] Slogan given to a woman to say during the second campaign against AIDS carried out by French television.

55

notions of Western religions. To be purified, one must be tested. Sexuality is sinful and sick; whatever restricts its practices basically represents a way to salvation. So, blessed be AIDS, which is supposed to deliver us from temptation, lead us to wisdom, and surreptitiously prevent a few births on the way!

If those affected by AIDS find some form of consolation and compensation for their suffering, then I'm glad. But if, for men who are said to be free, liberated, and not ill, AIDS appears to be the solution to our unsolved sexual problems, then it shows how underdeveloped our culture is in this matter. This underdevelopment might even be one of the causes of the spread of AIDS and several other modern diseases.

ILL FROM WHAT?

Indeed, people don't just become ill out of the blue. For the whole of a body to be affected, its equilibrium must have already been disrupted. That's true for all illnesses. It's painfully obvious for illnesses said to be of the immune system. But all illnesses are, in fact, since being ill comes down to being unable to distance oneself from pathogenic agents.

So why do we have this proliferation of terminal illnesses at a period of civilization as developed as ours? My hypothesis is that it's this very civilization that continuously submits our minds and bodies to stresses and strains and thus gradually destroys our immune systems. I'm surprised doctors aren't saying this. Are they being, in some way, unfaithful to the Hippocratic Oath? Might they have an interest in the spread of illness insofar as it's profitable? As it brings them financial or personal rewards? Or is it that they themselves are blind? Since they are so used to technological methods, do they still know what a healthy, living body is? Don't they wonder whether, for example, the constant stress caused by noise might well, among other things, make us prone to cancer, AIDS, etc., by weakening our biological, and especially hormonal, economy? Which could also make us sterile? Do you have to be a female psychotherapist to imagine this to be possible and to say it out loud?

To cure someone is fine, but prevention is better. Medical intervention in someone's life is a break-in to their world. In a way, it's a violation of their world that turns them into dependents. It also takes away their right to speak, because ill people often understand nothing of the medical jargon or reasoning behind a particular diagnosis or treatment.

RESOUNDING SEXUAL POWER

Doctor-patient relationships somewhat resemble the sexual power relations that still hold sway for many couples. Which isn't to cast doubt upon doctors' professionalism, but rather upon sexual education; this isn't only a private affair but something that concerns social relations in general.

Take the right to make noise, materially or spiritually, which is a man's privilege. Most of them are only finally satisfied once they can play about with noisy machines in front of others, particularly women. Their social discontent fades away at the wheel of a vehicle, its sonorous performance conveying the proof of their sexual power. Imagine machines that no longer emitted any sound at all: men would be forced to undergo a far more worthwhile sexual reeducation than that which AIDS has necessitated. And what I would suggest to today's mothers is not that they teach girls to be like boys, but rather that they bring up boys to be capable of the same social virtues as girls, while at the same time being men sexually: to

57

know how to remain silent, calm, and to speak quietly, to keep from playing noisy and warlike games, to be attentive to others, modest and patient, and so on.

Respecting these cultural customs, which often amounts to nothing more than simply being polite, wouldn't do the economy of male sexuality any harm. On the contrary, it would help prevent its energy being dissipated in those social stereotypes which our recent findings on sexuality could render null and void. Today, sophisticated sexual practice ought to be distinguishable from the use of a weapon, from noisy exhibitionism, from speaking arrogantly, claiming to be right, using theory in a bellicose way, etc.

Our sexual liberations should imperceptibly change our sociocultural environment. Machines handled by men ought not to make more noise than those tolerated in a woman's hands. Curiously enough, whereas the one sort invade all areas of our existence, the others aren't supposed to go beyond the walls of a well-built house. In the same way, then, conflicts between men or their peoples should be able to be dealt with politely, amicably, or at least without subjecting women and children to noise or harm.

A TRULY FREE SEXUALITY

No doubt most people will think I'm joking in saying all this. But not at all. Without doubt it is hard to imagine to what extent all these ways of behaving that are typical of politics and govern so-called civil behavior, that swallow up massive amounts of money and pollute our environment with military defenses, and that currently threaten our lives and our physical and moral health, are the result of peculiar sexual games between men. Unfortunately, for centuries they have constituted the framework of our lives. It's unfortunate, too, that when it comes to life, our civilizations have a habit of destroying what they have gained. This economy bears a strange resemblance to the masculine sexual economy described by Freud: tension, discharge, return to homoeostasis. But this economy lays down our law, everywhere, all the time; it makes us ill, either directly or indirectly, and through medical science as well.

One way out of this cultural landscape that corresponds to what is said to be the sole, and masculine (or at best neutral) sexuality would certainly be to bring up boys differently and thus modify the social behavior of men. This measure I feel is especially necessary given that the perpetual denunciation of war is accompanied by a proliferation of warlike toys and games, and by aggressive public images and behavior, which do nothing to bring about peace and clarity in the minds of either children or adults.

Developing your sexuality doesn't involve reproducing (one more) child but rather transforming your sexual energy with a view to a pleasurable and fertile cohabitation with others. Society shouldn't demand the repression of our sexual desires, their denial or nullification, or that we keep them in their infancy or a state of animality. Rather, they should be incorporated into an individual and collective subjectivity capable of respect for oneself, persons of one's own and the other sex, an entire people, and peoples in general. How far we are from achieving that! To call on illness to resolve our problems, to destroy subjectivity as one breaks a plaything or a culture out of pique or impotence, is to make naive and irresponsible sexual gestures.

October 1987

8

LINGUISTIC SEXES AND GENDERS

Women's entry into the public world, the social relations they have among themselves and with men, have made cultural transformations, and especially linguistic ones, a necessity. If the male President of the Republic meets the Queen, to say *Ils se sont rencontrés* (they met) borders on a grammatical anomaly.[1] Instead of dealing with this difficult question, most people wonder whether it wouldn't be better if we were governed by just men or just women, that is, by one gender alone. The

[1] Irigaray is referring to the rule of using the masculine plural in French whenever masculine and feminine are combined (see 3. "Women's Discourse and Men's Discourse," p. 22), according primacy to the masculine, which in this case might be seen to contradict the social custom of according primacy to the one having majesty over the "ordinary" subject or citizen (even elected presidents). (Tr.)

rules of language have so strong a bearing on things that they can lead to such impasses. Unfortunately, there's still little appreciation of what's at stake here. Faced with the need to transform the rules of grammar, some women, even feminists—though fortunately not all—readily object that provided they have the right to use it, the masculine gender will do for them. But neutralizing grammatical gender amounts to an abolition of the difference between sexed subjectivities and to an increasing exclusion of a culture's sexuality. We would be taking a huge step backwards if we abolished grammatical gender, a step our civilization can ill afford; what we do need, on the other hand, and it's essential, is for men and women to have equal subjective rights—equal obviously meaning different but of equal value, subjective implying equivalent rights in exchange systems. From a linguistic perspective, therefore, the cultural injustices of language and its generalized sexism have to be analyzed. These are to be found in grammar, in vocabulary, in the connotations of a word's gender.

MORE OR LESS MASCULINE

For centuries, whatever has been valorized has been masculine in gender, whatever devalorized, feminine. So the sun is masculine, and the moon feminine. Yet in our cultures, *le soleil* (the sun) is thought of as the source of life, *la lune* (the moon) as ambiguous, almost harmful, except perhaps by some peasants. The attribution of masculine gender to the sun can be traced in History, and so can the attribution of the sun to the men-gods. These aren't all immutable truths but rather facts that evolve over long periods of time and at different rates of speed depending upon the culture, country, and language. The positive connotation of the masculine as word gender derives from the time of the establishment of patriarchal and phallocratic power, notably by men's appropriation of the divine. This is not a secondary matter. It is very important. Without divine power, men could not have supplanted mother–daughter relations and their attributions concerning nature and society. But man becomes God by giving himself an invisible father, a father language. Man becomes God as the Word, then as the Word made flesh. Because the power of semen isn't immediately obvious in procreation, it's relayed by the linguistic code, the *logos*. Which wants to become the all-embracing truth.

Men's appropriation of the linguistic code attempts to do at least three things:

1. prove they are fathers;
2. prove they are more powerful than mother-women;
3. prove they are capable of engendering the cultural domain as they have been engendered in the natural domain of the ovum, the womb, the body of a woman.

To guarantee loyalty to its authority, the male people consciously or unconsciously represents whatever has value as corresponding to its image and its grammatical gender. Most linguists state that grammatical gender is arbitrary, independent of sexual denotations and connotations. In fact, this is untrue. They haven't really thought about the issue. It doesn't strike them as being important. Their personal subjectivity, their theory is content to be valorized like the masculine, passing for an arbitrary universal. A patient study of the gender of words almost always reveals their hidden sex. Rarely is this immediately apparent. And a linguist will be quick to retort that *un fauteuil* (a sofa) or *un chateau* (a castle) are not more "masculine" than *une chaise* (a chair) or *une maison* (a house). Apparently not. A degree of thought will show that the former connote greater value than the latter. While the latter are simply useful in our cultures, the others are more luxurious, ornamental, noted for their distinction as higher-class goods. A thorough analysis of all the terms of the lexicon would in this way make their secret sex apparent, signifying their adherence to an as yet uninterpreted syntax. Another example: *un ordinateur* (a computer) is of course a masculine noun and *la machine à écrire* (the typewriter) a feminine one. Value is what matters . . . Whatever has it must be masculine. Again, *un avion* (an airplane) is superior to *une voiture* (a car), *le Boeing* to *la Caravelle*, not to mention *le Concorde* . . . With each counterexample we find a more complex explanation: the gender could be due to the prefix or the suffix and not to the root of the word; it could depend upon the time when the term entered the lexicon and the relative value of the masculine and feminine genders then (in this respect, Italian is a less coherently sexist language than French); sometimes its determination is consequent upon the language it's borrowed from (English, for example, gives us a number of terms that become masculine in French).

GENDER AS IDENTITY OR AS POSSESSION

How is gender attributed to words? It's done on different levels and in different ways. At the most archaic level, I think there is an identification of the denominated reality with the sex of the speaking subject. *La terre* (the earth) *is* woman, *le ciel* (the sky) *is* her brother. *Le soleil* (the sun) *is* man, the god-man. *La lune* (the moon) is woman, sister of the man-god. And so

---

on. Something of this first identification always remains in the gender of words. The degree to which it is explicit or hidden varies. But there is another mechanism at work apart from the identification of designated reality and gender. Living beings, the animate and cultured, become masculine; objects that are lifeless, the inanimate and uncultured, become feminine. Which means that men have attributed subjectivity to themselves and have reduced women to the status of objects, or to nothing. This is as true for actual women as it is for the gender of words. Le moissonneur (a harvester) is a man. But if, in line with current debate on the names of occupations, a linguist or legislator wishes to name a woman who harvests la moissonneuse,[2] the word is not available for a female subject: la moissonneuse (harvesting machine) is the tool the male harvester makes use of, or else it doesn't exist in the feminine. This state of affairs is even more ridiculous at a higher professional level where sometimes one is presented with hierarchies in the attribution of grammatical gender: le secrétaire d'Etat/parti (the secretary of state or a party) is masculine and la secrétaire steno-dactylo (the shorthand secretary) is feminine.

There is no sexed couple to create and structure the world. Men are surrounded by tools of feminine gender and by women-objects. Men don't manage the world with women as sexed subjects having equivalent rights. Only through a transformation of language will that become possible. But this transformation can only take place if we valorize the feminine gender once more. Indeed, the feminine, which was originally just different, is now practically assimilated to the non-masculine. Being a woman is equated with not being a man. Which is what psychoanalysis calmly informs us in its theory

[2] The suffix euse designates a feminine term. (Tr.)

and its practice of penis or phallus envy. Its reality only corresponds to one cultural period and one state of language. In that case, the way for women to be liberated is not by "becoming a man" or by envying what men have and their objects, but by female subjects once again valorizing the expression of their own sex and gender. That's completely different.

This confusion between liberation as equal ownership of goods and liberation as access to a subjectivity of the same value is currently upheld by several social theories and practices: psychoanalysis is one of them, but another is Marxism, to a certain extent. These discourses have been elaborated by men. They used Germanic languages. At the present time they have a relative degree of success among women in countries that speak these languages, because gender is expressed in subject-object relations. In these languages a woman can therefore have *her* (*sa*) phallus if not *her* (*sa*) penis.[3] Thus some German, English, or American women are able, for example, to demand equality in relation to the possession of goods and mark them with their gender. Having achieved this, they may abandon their right to denote gender in relation to the subject and criticize the conscious relationship made between the sexuate body and language as "materialist," "ontological," "idealist," etc. This shows a lack of comprehension of the relations between individual bodies, social bodies, and the linguistic economy. A great deal of misunderstanding in the so-called world of women's liberation is perpetuated by

---

[3] In French the possessive adjective agrees in gender (and number) with the object possessed rather than with the possessor, as in English. To illustrate the point of her comparison Irigaray uses the possessive adjective for feminine singular nouns, *sa*, instead of the masculine *son*, for the masculine nouns *phallus* and *penis*.

this lack of comprehension. For many an Anglo-Saxon—and in general Germanic language—feminist, all she needs is her university post or to have written her book to be liberated. For them it's a question of her (*sa*) post and her (*sa*) book[4] and this appropriation of ownership seems to satisfy them. In my view, we have to be free female *subjects*. Language represents an essential tool of production for this liberation. I have to make it progress in order to have subjective rights equivalent to men, to be able to exchange language and objects with them. For one women's liberation movement, the emphasis is on equal rights in relation to the possession of goods: difference between men and women is located in the nature, the quantity, and sometimes the quality of goods acquired and possessed. For the other movement, sexual liberation means to demand access to a status of individual and collective *subjectivity* that is valid for them as women. The emphasis is on the difference of rights between male and female subjects.

THE SEX OF OCCUPATIONS

Owning a few goods equivalent to those men have doesn't solve the problem of gender for women who speak Romance languages because these goods don't bear the mark of their owner's subject. We say *mon enfant* (my child) or *mon phallus* (?) (my phallus) whether we are men or women. For valuable "objects," then, the mark of ownership is the same. As for other "objects," they are generally devalorized when they are likely to be used or appropriated by women alone. The

---

[4] University post (*poste universitaire*) and book (*livre*) are masculine, hence Irigaray here again replaces the masculine possessive adjective with the feminine one. (Tr.)

---

problem of the object and its conquest cannot therefore solve the problem of inequality of sexed rights in all languages. Furthermore, I don't think it can solve it in any language. But it can just about satisfy demands, more or less immediately.

If the issue of names for occupations has been taken up so extensively, it's because such names represent an intermediary space between subject and object, object and subject. Of course, it is a matter of possessing professional status, having a job, but this cannot be possessed just like any object can. It represents a necessary, though not sufficient, part of subjective identity. In addition, this demand fits in well with the social demands already being made in the male world. Therefore, the issue is relatively easy to raise. People generally go along with it. Often its only opposition is reality as it has already been coded linguistically (so *moissonneuse* and *médecine* have become the names of objects or designate a professional discipline and are no longer names for people, and sometimes the female name for an occupation doesn't exist or designates a different job[5]) and social resistance depending upon the level of access available for women. But in this debate about the names of occupations the issue of language's sexism has hardly been broached, and proposed solutions often tend to try to skirt around the problems it raises.

October 1987

[5] See 15. "The Cost of Words," p. 112. (Tr.)

9

THE RIGHT TO LIFE

"Shocked by Chernobyl, 70 to 80 percent of Italians have declared themselves against nuclear power." That's how I heard the results of the Italian referendum announced.[1] Long-wave interference prevented me, at first, from knowing what Italian women and men had decided regarding the power of judges. I would have liked to have had both results. I only heard one of them and with that concluded that this must be a sick country.

I don't really think that. But if my sympathies for Italy allow me this comparison, the analysis of nuclear culture that I put forward, in part, at the Italian Communist Party's Women's Festival in 1986 (cf. "Une chance de vivre" in Sexes and parentés [2]) earned me just such an assessment from some of the media. It would appear that I'm "afraid" of technological progress. . . .

[1] November 1987 referendum on: 1. nuclear power; 2. judicial power.
[2] Op. cit.; also in Temps de la Différence (Paris: Biblio Essais, 1989).

POLITICAL RESPONSIBILITY

I think that to stick the label of a mental or physical illness on a life-protecting political option shows an astonishing lack of awareness. To me it also appears to be a sign of an imperialistic form of reason related to the unconditional power of money. It would seem that being in good health is a matter of declaring oneself in favor of a rather blind development of the means of profit. What does it matter, ultimately, that there will no longer be anyone here to benefit; the most important thing would be to prove that profit was the intention. Thus, one can discern that concern for human lives is no big thing in the context of a currency war where victory is thought to depend upon the expansion of various technologies. It's not unthinkable, either, that the excessive praise given to advanced medicines works to the detriment of preventive medicines. The cult of medical or biological discoveries seems to disregard: 1. the day-to-day hazards of our culture; 2. the damage caused by medicine itself. The only response to this claim I've been able to get from supposedly intelligent people is: it was no better in the past. . . .

In the Italian referendum, I thought it was precisely the right to life that brought the two issues in question together. The need for a popular vote shows how inadequate civil rights are in relation to the protection of life these days. But how can it be forbidden for individuals to kill or steal if the State itself kills or steals? Who will be empowered as judges if those who govern the nation cannot themselves be? How can the rights and obligations of everyone, women and men, be redefined in this complex culture for which written law makes no provision? On what basis are those in charge going to justify their verdicts? On a religious basis? Which religion? Which country is currently tributary to a single religion? And who would want to revive the edicts of patriarchal monotheisms regarding female rights?

A NEW OPIATE OF THE PEOPLE?

It is obvious that the most immediately important issue is the right to life. Many changes and additions to the law concerning property relations have been introduced in the last few decades. It's true that the degree of their enforcement varies, especially in the matter of sexual discrimination. Theoretically, women enjoy certain rights that they did not previously have regarding the acquisition or ownership of property. But this progress, insufficient and fragile as it is, can only be consolidated if it is accompanied by the right to life, a right which is always sexed. Indeed, life is not neuter. And to assert that men and women are now equal or well on the way to becoming so has served almost as an opiate of the people for some time now. Men and women are not equal, and I think it's very problematic or misguided to orient development in this direction. Take the work context, for example, where an employer will be quick to claim that the reason he doesn't want a female workforce is because of women's lack of emotional stability. Or he will agree to take them on provided he can underpay them, failing to recognize that women are often the most profitable workforce given their reliability, especially later on in life.

I fail to see how a woman can pass for a man at work. She can, of course, dress like a man, stop making love or doing the housework, no longer have children, change her voice, etc. Something of the sort occurs from time to time as a symptom of the neutralization of the sexes in modern times. What should be asked is whether this is due to the choice of particular women or to the necessities of a world men construct, a world women do not choose but tolerate. They do not become women; they become men. This is what the male world demands of them by failing to recognize female identity.

WOMEN OUTSIDE THE FAMILY

How can this be valorized? What would seem essential is to write female rights into civil law. Women need specific rights. We still live in a framework of familio-religious relations in which the woman is the body to the man's head. It's quite astonishing that men, who in their cradle were totally dependent upon women and who owe their existence to this dependence, should then take the liberty of turning things around: men exist thanks to women's intelligence, but apparently women aren't capable of governing society nor even of being full citizens. This reversal of confidence is worth a closer look. It smacks of competitiveness, even revenge. Obviously, men are prepared to say that a mother knows how to look after the material, nonspiritual side of things and that women are better at it than they are. They have never been mothers . . . This job requires more subtlety and intelligence than any other. It would certainly be done better if women had the full benefit of their identity. But, to date, those who engender and protect life don't have a right to it. In an incredibly distrustful maneuver, it's suspected that they would no longer want to protect life the moment they themselves have a right to it. Women are often nothing more than hostages of the reproduction of the species. Their right to life requires them to have legal authority over their body and their subjectivity.

All the following issues of women's lives ought to made

the concern of and written into civil law: temporary conces-
sions on contraception and abortion; partial and provisional
protection from and penalties against public and domestic
violence against women; the abuse of female bodies for the
purpose of pornography or advertising; discrimination in the
sexist definition and use of the body, of images, of language;
rape, kidnapping, murder, and the exploitation of children
who are—it seems it has to be repeated—the fruit of female,
not made, labor, etc. These are only a few examples of what
has to be legally specified in order to define women's life as
citizens.

Otherwise, who are we? What value do words still have
given such distortions of reality? Women, it's said, have joined
men in enjoying civil rights. Who considers the fact that they
have no identity in public life? Their identity was defined only
in relation to the family. It has to be rethought as the identity
of half of humankind: the female gender. Humankind, in fact,
doesn't only reproduce the species. It's comprised of two
equally creative genders, one of which is, additionally, a pro-
creator in itself, in its body. That doesn't stop it from having
the right to freedom, identity, and spirit. Before (re)pro-
ducing again and without yet knowing where it's going,
humankind should consider its double-poled identity and
inscribe the richness of its life properties into culture.

A CULTURE OF LIFE

Life is worth much more than all the objects, property, and
riches imaginable. Is it not a sign that the blindness of some
is meeting resistance if a whole people remembers this? It
sometimes seems as if Italians lack gravity in view of world's
serious problems. But what if Italian men (very much with

the help of Italian women . . .) were right to protest against the pursuit of profit to the detriment of life? After all, in the midst of all its crises that no one takes seriously, Italy is getting along better than many other countries, and the people still know how to make plain their will to live. It only remains for them to make plain that life is sexuate, that gender neutralization puts us, individually and collectively, in danger of death. In order to affirm this as historical progress, it is important to elaborate an as yet nonexistent sexual culture that respects the two genders.

It is quite simply a matter of social justice to balance out the power one sex or gender has over the other by giving or giving back subjective and objective rights to women, rights appropriate to their sexed bodies.

Justice in the right to life cannot be exercised without a culture of humankind comprising men and women, and written law defining civil rights and obligations that correspond to their respective identities. In this respect, we're still in the infancy of History. Fortunately!

November 1987

10

WHY DEFINE SEXED RIGHTS?

Christina Lasagni: *Why are you now taking an interest in law, especially as you have approached problems in such a different way before?* [1]

Luce Irigaray: As a philosopher, I am interested in theorizing all domains of reality and knowledge. Only very recently in the history of culture have philosophy and the sciences been separated—the result of methodological specialization, making them beyond the reach of anyone and everyone. The hypertechnical tendencies of current science lead to the creation of increasingly complex formulae that correspond, so it's believed, to an increasingly truthful truth. Consequently, it's a truth that escapes consideration in the light of wisdom, the scientist's own included. This doesn't bode well for our

[1] Christina Lasagni asked me these questions for the first issue of Il diritto delle donne, journal of Emilia Romagna, published in Bologna, Italy.

culture and its future development (cf. on this subject, "Sujet de la Science, Sujet Sexué?" in *Sens et place des connaissances dans la societé*).[2]

So I have always been concerned with the issue of law from the perspective of the difference between the sexes. In *Speculum*, for instance, I discuss it quite explicitly on pages 148–54 and 266–81 [of the French edition], but it pervades the whole chapter on Plato. In *This Sex Which Is Not One*,[3] two chapters—"Women on the Market" and "Commodities Among Themselves"—consider the problems of economic and social rights. I'm dealing with the question in a more concrete way now. But as far as I'm concerned, there is no break between my earlier and latest texts, especially in this matter.

Why deal with legal questions more concretely? Because since 1970 I have regularly worked with women or groups of women who belong to liberation movements, and in these I've observed problems or impasses that can't be resolved except through the establishment of an equitable legal system for both sexes. In the absence of such social structures, women and men are losing themselves in spiraling demands, legal or otherwise, while in the meantime there's no protection for the basic rights of every individual and global disorder increases. So the reestablishment of a pseudo-order is sought through the restoration of order to another country by nations incapable of managing their own problems. It's better to give aid than to leave people to die. But is it really a question of aid? Or is it a more a question of apparently generous alibis

[2] "Is the subject of science sexed?" trans. Carol Mastrangelo Bové, *Hypatia* 2 (Fall 1987): 65–87.

[3] Trans. Catherine Porter with Carolyn Burke (Ithaca: Cornell University Press, 1985), originally published (Paris: Minuit, 1977).

in order to remain masters of the situation? It's not clear. And the laws of most use to us here and now, those to do with us, are always put off as if the world had grown accustomed to disorder, and in this quasi-deluge of our civilizations, all we have to do is find a way of rescuing man's identity—without taking any notice of the civilization women transmit. Any old excuse will do for not taking account of their truth. Men are even going back to archaic stages of culture by forcing their largely domesticated animals on the public as their latest totem. Instead of pursuing cultural development, the world is retreating to the minimum grounds for human definition. The consequences are that we no longer have any religion appropriate for our times, nor complete control of language as a tool of social exchange, or as a means to acquire or create knowledge. Our legislation is not adequate to regulate private, religious, national, and international conflicts, particularly when it comes to the protection of life. Therefore, we no longer have any God(s), any language, any familiar cultural landscape . . . What do we have, then, to base social groups upon? I know some people think that the great eve of universal well-being has arrived. But which universal? What new imperialism is there lurking in all this? And who will pay the price for it? There is no universal valid for all men and women aside from the natural economy. All other universals are partial constructions and, as a result, authoritarian and unjust. The first universal to establish would be legislation valid for both sexes as a basic element of human culture. That doesn't mean enforcing sexual choices. But we are "living" women and men, that is to say sexuate, and our identity can't be constructed without the benefit of a framework of relations, horizontal and vertical, that respects this difference.

In the absence of such an order, many people are nowadays looking for an identity-space other than the human one. A man defines himself in relation to his house or his neighbor's, his car or any other means of transport, the number of miles he's covered, the number of matches he's played, his favorite animals, his unique Gods in whose name he kills others and looks down on women, and so on. Man doesn't concern himself with improving the quality of man: "Oh, I've got no time for that . . . That's old-fashioned . . . It's a thing of the past, that is . . ." All these indifferent responses, expressed passively by irresponsible citizens, are in my view the result of a lack of rights and obligations appropriate to real civil persons. Which leads to a great deal of authoritarianism, violence, and poverty.

C. L.:   *You talk about law that is sexed, law that encompasses female gender. It's a very different idea from the traditional notion of "parity." So it's not a matter of "equal laws for all" but rather a notion of law that takes into account the fact that women are not equal to men. Can you explain the concept of sexed law?*

L. I.:   I think that, in particular cases, the struggle has to be for equal rights in order to make the differences between women and men apparent. Or at least I used to think that. I now think that what appears to be the reasonable way is utopian or misguided. Why? Women and men are not equal. And the strategy of equality, when there is one,[4] should always aim to get differences recognized. For example, having equal numbers of men and women in all sectors of social activity in order to get them to progress. Of course, on one

---

[4] And it's present in the very concept of law, though not simply as a strategy.

---

level this is a totally desirable solution. But it's not enough. And it's this insufficiency that brings about repression and uncertainty concerning the differences between men and women, which women themselves maintain. Why is the equality strategy not enough? First, because the current social order, and that includes the order defining occupations, is not neutral when viewed in terms of the difference of the sexes. Working conditions and production techniques are not equally designed nor equally applied with respect to sexual difference. Working targets and systems are not equally defined by, nor for, women and men. At best, therefore, equality is achieved on pay. Of course, the right to equal pay is legitimate, as is the right of women to work outside the home and gain economic independence. Some people (men and women) think that this is sufficient in order to respect their human identity. Personally, I don't think it is. These new economic conditions can encourage us to rethink the whole of our social organization, unless they give support to the fact that, in order to achieve a minimum of freedom, women have to subject themselves to the imperatives of a culture that is not their own. Hence, should they have to help manufacture armaments or pollutants, or adjust themselves to men's working patterns, or again should they have to submit and contribute to the development of artificial languages unrelated to their natural language, which increasingly depersonalizes them, and so on? That doesn't equate with having equal rights. Because to have a chance of living freely, women are forced to subject themselves to men's means of production and to enhance their capital or sociocultural inheritance. In spite of all this they do enter the workplace, but in so doing they alienate their female identity. And the incentives that exist for women to go back into the home have a good chance of success, not necessarily among the most reactionary women, as is too readily believed, but also among women who wish to try to become women. What I mean by that is that there is still hardly any sort of work that enables a woman to earn her living as a male citizen does without alienating her identity in working conditions and contexts developed to suit men alone. Not considering this problem causes a great deal of misunderstanding and disagreement among people working for women's liberation. A good deal of time is lost in the mistakes that are made, and many misunderstandings are fostered, cynically or unknowingly, by those in power on a micro or macro level. As for women themselves, they are caught in a dilemma: stuck between the minimum social rights they can obtain by going out to work, gaining economic independence, being seen somewhat in society, etc., and the psychological or physical price they pay, and make other women pay, for this minimum, whether they are totally aware of it or not. All these misunderstandings could be resolved by the recognition that different laws exist for each sex and that equivalent social status can only be established after these laws have been encoded by civil society's elected representatives. So this must be aimed at as a priority.

C. L.: *Can you give some examples, in order to explain how current law was created and has developed to suit men? What laws would be created in accordance with sexual difference?*

L. I.: I think it's possible for me to answer both questions at once, in the sense that what has to be defined as women's rights is what the male people, the between-men culture, has appropriated as possessions, including in this respect not only women's and children's bodies, but also natural space, living space, the economy of signs and images, social and religious representation.

I'll deal with the question, then, by way of what has to be asserted now as women's rights:

1. The right to *human dignity*, which means:

    (a) Stopping the commercial use of their bodies and images
    (b) Valid representations of themselves in actions, words, and images in all public places
    (c) Stopping the exploitation of motherhood, a functional part of women, by civil and religious powers.

2. The right to *human identity*, that is:

    (a) The legal encodification of virginity (or physical and moral integrity) as a component of female identity that is not reducible to money, and not cash-convertible by the family, the State, or religious bodies in any way. This component of female identity enables the girl to be accorded civil status and gives her a right to keep her virginity (including for her own relationship with the divine) as long as she likes, as well as to lodge a complaint, with the support of the law, against anyone who violates this right from within or outside the family. If it is true that girls are less the objects of exchange between men in our cultures, there are still plenty of places where their virginity is traded, and girls' identity status as a cash-convertible body between men has been neither reformulated nor rethought. Girls need a positive identity to refer to as individual and social civil persons. Such an autonomous identity for girls is also essential for the free consent of women to sexual relationships and for the institution of marriage if women are not to be alienated by male power.

What's more, this institution should be legally modified, especially in relation to the marriage of minors. At the moment, the law allows the family, the State, or religious bodies to be the legal guardians of the young married couple, and especially the woman, who can be married well before she reaches the age of majority. In my opinion we should increase the age of legal marriage or reduce that of civil majority and not allow marriage to operate as, in effect, an uncivil institution—that is, without the couple being in any way legally responsible.

These rights would enable us to get away from simple penal sanctions and to enjoy civil legality as far as women's rights are concerned. I'm thinking of rape and incest cases, for example, or cases against forced prostitution, pornography, etc., which are always enacted with a view to punishing the guilty rather than in accordance with civil society's guarantee of positive rights appropriate to women. But it's not a good thing, either for women or for relations between the sexes, that women as the injured party be put in the position of simply being accusers. If there were civil rights for women, the whole of society would be the injured party in the case of rape or all the other forms of violence inflicted on women; society, then, would be the plaintiff or co-plaintiff against the harm caused to one of its members.

(b) The right to *motherhood* as a component (not a priority) of female identity. If the body is a legal concern, and it is, then the female body must be civilly identified as a virgin and potential mother. Which means the mother will have the right to choose whether to be pregnant and the number of pregnancies. The mother herself, or her legal representative, will be the one to register the child's birth with the civil authorities.

3. The mutual obligations of mothers-children shall be defined by civil law. This is so that the mother can protect her children and be supported in this by law. That will enable her to be the plaintiff in the name of civil society in incest, rape, abuse, and kidnapping cases concerning children, particularly girls. The respective obligations of the mother and the father will be defined separately.

4. Women shall have a right to defend their own and their children's lives, their living space, their traditions, and their religion against all unilateral decisions emanating from male law (including in this respect armaments and pollution).

5. On a strictly financial level:

   (a) Celibacy shall not be penalized by the tax system nor any other charges.
   (b) If the State grants family benefits, they shall be of equal value for each child.
   (c) Media broadcasts, such as television, for which women pay the same taxes as men, shall be half of the time targeted towards women.

6. Systems of exchange, such as linguistic exchange, for example, shall be revised in order to guarantee a right to equivalent exchange for men and women.

---

7. Women shall be represented in equal numbers in all civil and religious decision-making bodies, given that religion also represents civil authority.

C. L.: *Some women have theorized their exteriority and aversion to law, their lack of interest in these issues. What do you think of this?*

L. I.: I think this position is a poor analysis of what are the current conditions for the recognition of female identity. But I can appreciate that these women—kept by men-citizens (who generally use law in a way that is foreign to female interests) and not being citizens in their own right—forget this essential dimension of the social structure. I can particularly understand it given that, at the time when female law existed, it wasn't generally written and was exercised without the weight of the institutions that have proliferated under patriarchal regimes. But this female law did exist. The era when women governed the social order did not end in chaos, as some claim. Among other things, female law was characterized by:

1. The transmission of possessions and names between mothers and daughters
2. The privilege of sisters and of the last-born in a later transmission
3. The significance of divinity and the religious in filiation
4. The designation of the country of birth as the motherland
5. Respect for local places and divinities
6. Respect for naturally produced food: fruits most of all, then cereals
7. A temporality that respects the rhythms of life, the light cycle, the seasons, and the years

———

8. A higher morality based upon love and peace
9. A community of all the members of humankind
10. Arbitration entrusted to women on matters of alliances and the resolution of conflicts
11. Symbolic systems linked to art

One can find traces of these elements of female law in the works of Johann Jacob Bachofen, as well as in Mircea Eliade's descriptions of aboriginal cultures that still exist in India, for example. These references are far from being exclusive. They, and their bibliographies, may be able to provide a lead for research. I have chosen to cite men partly to illustrate male theorists' recognition of this reality.

In order for these rights to be respected today, rights that seem to me to correspond to female subjectivity, we will have to resort to written law. Otherwise, written law will continue to be enforced to the detriment of girls, who are alienated from it from birth and by their genealogies. Moreover, I think it would be a good thing for women to create a social order in which they can make use of their subjectivity with its symbols, its images, its dreams and realities—thus, the objective means of subjective exchange.

C. L.: *I'd like to finish off this interview by asking you for some advice for women (and men, too) who are interested in the law.*

L. I.: As a priority, they should guarantee the conservation of nature insofar as it's what enables everyone to live and feed themselves through work without speculative and alienating mediations.

1. Specify the basic rights for everyone's life: women and

men, girls and boys, mothers and fathers, female and male citizens, women and men workers, etc., starting with women and men, or at least retaining this difference as a framework if other priorities come to the fore.

2. Reduce the rights of groups or companies governed by one or only a few people. Democracy itself still does not exist in the sense in which it is invoked, and its principles need to be looked at, particularly in the light of the time and manner in which it was defined and established by men alone.

3. Redefine and value adequate laws on housing, and indeed private property in general. Women, men, and children need a place to live without being cheated of this need, this desire, this rightful investment, by environmental pollution (cars, airplanes, noisy machines, etc.), by lack of safety or faulty construction, liberties taken in building places initially denied permission to be built, and therefore depriving existing residents of light, air, and peace, and forcing them into a semi-nomadism through a lack of legal protection regarding real estate.

4. Reduce the power money has, particularly the surplus value associated with the capricious desires of the rich or those not so rich (take, for example, real estate agents who speculate on human greed by pretending that a smaller apartment can be more expensive since it's sought after by purchasers having trouble moving, but the sellers know that's not the case), and get back to valid exchanges based on the cost of products and the choice of means of production (which means going back to more natural methods without increasing production or overproducing with respect to the earth, the air, the oceans, and human bodies, too).

---

5. Question the origins of the law currently in force, particularly in relation to the time when women really were civil persons, a time misleadingly termed Prehistory. This will lead you to consider what has to be changed in current law and to question the notions of the civil and the religious as assimilable or differentiated and guaranteeing free choices.

May 1988

11

"MORE WOMEN THAN MEN"[1]

Luce Irigaray: I appreciate the sincerity of your contribution to public debate in your article *"Le penseur neutre était une femme"* [2] and the fact that in it you openly question yourself. I think you will make many women aware of how they behave without realizing it. It shows that what you describe as your own story—the supposedly "neutral" path you took and your conversion to the feminine—is not only your own but also that

---

[1] Manifesto published by the women's bookshop in Milan—a women's group to which Luisa Muraro belongs—in *Sottosopra vert*, 1985. For further elaboration of the issues and the perspective formulated in this pamphlet, see *Sexual Difference: A Theory of Social-Symbolic Practice*, trans. Patricia Cicogna and Teresa de Lauretis (Bloomington: Indiana University Press, 1990). Originally published as *Non credere di avere dei diritti: la generazione della libertà femminile nell'idea e nelle vicende di un gruppo di donne*, The Milan Women's Bookstore Collective (Turin: Rosenberg and Sellier, 1987). (Tr.)
[2] Cf. "Le sexe linguistique," *op. cit.*

---

of a good number of women in our culture. Your realization and public account of it will mean that people will no longer be able so authoritatively to assert the "neutral" position as the way to liberate women. Therefore, I can and want to go a little further with you, as clearly we share some assumptions: we necessarily have to be sexed female subjects. Which is an ethical matter, too, with respect to other women, our mothers and sisters, whether natural or spiritual. Given this necessity, which is not only an empirical one but a choice we make to become women subjectively, I'd like to ask you a few questions about some of the assertions you make in this article and in others you've published.

L. I.:   You and a number of other women have called for the right to "verticality" in female identity. Can you comment upon the meaning of this demand so it's not confused with the interpretation often attributed to this word in phallocratic cultures? In other words, can you explain how, according to particular passages in your article, this word signifies for you:

1. a woman's right to her genealogical becoming, a right you have had taken from you, you explain, causing both your own distress and an unintentioned lack of fairness on your part vis-á-vis your mother and other women?
2. women's right to their own spiritual becoming, a right in harmony with their sexed body instead of one that denies it in the name of an allegedly universal and neutral truth?

So, can you explain how in your opinion—and in mine—the object of women's liberation is not to become the "super-women" of a culture that now exploits us in this way, but rather to find an identity that can't be reduced to motherhood, to

---

being "just like men," or to being good little performers, like machines.

Luisa Muraro: The idea of a necessary dimension of verticality comes from Carla Lonzi[3] (who in fact talks of female transcendence), from Simone Weil's *Cahiers*, and from your *Ethique de la Différence Sexuelle*.[4] The phallic signification of verticality too often leads us to forget that solar energy moves in a vertical direction, that the force of gravity is vertical, just as the direction of sap and vegetable life in general is too. We are dealing, of course, with partially figurative language, a double signification that is often found in what you yourself say. Like other women, like every other woman, perhaps, I came into the world with the desire to be "grown up" (*grande*),[5] meaning an adult, certainly, but not only that. And I found a society in which all notions of being grown up (*grandeur*), apart from physiological development, seemed to belong to the other sex. That threw me into *confusion*, about both my desires and my female identity. I couldn't manage to square the one with the other, and it was even more difficult for me see to it that they fed into one another.

---

[3] An Italian woman whose publications include most notably her essay *Sputtiamo su Hegel*.

[4] *The Notebooks of Simone Weil*, in two volumes (London: Routledge and Kegan Paul, 1956), originally published as *Cahiers* in three volumes (Paris: Plon, 1951, 1953, 1956). *The Ethics of Sexual Difference*, trans. Carolyn Burke (Ithaca: Cornell University Press, forthcoming), originally published as *Ethique de la Différence Sexuelle* (Paris: Minuit, 1984).

[5] *Grand(e)* has multiple meanings, including "big," "grown up," "fully grown," but also "great" in the sense of having magnitude, being significant, having magnanimity and splendor. Hence *grandeur* not only signifies size, but also greatness and importance. (Tr.)

At the moment, I'm working to make possible this enriching circularity between female identity and the desires a woman may have. I'm working toward a society in which, for instance, a female love(r) of knowledge has a figurative and a concrete meaning at the same time. Well, that goes beyond the minimum freedom that we take for granted each woman wants for herself. I want for myself and for others freedom that's rooted in my gender; many women have given up the search for this or they've never even tried to find it. One has to be clear about it.

L. I.: The *Sottosopra vert* manifesto (Milan, 1985) defined *self-assurance* (*l'aise*)[6] as a goal of women's liberation. In this there was, I think, something very pertinent, and yet it showed both strength and naïveté, in that:

1. In society, compromises always have to be made. It's rarely a place to be self-assured. Being together demands reciprocal respect and consideration.
2. Women cannot be self-assured without language and systems of representation being transformed, because these are appropriate to men's subjectivity; they are reassuring to the between-men culture. In raising these questions, I obviously don't want to quash your initiative, which is a good thing, as many women have found it encouraging. I want to suggest that you, we, continue our efforts with the understanding that women cannot find assurance in

---

[6] *L'aise* also has multiple meanings; it can mean "pleasure" and "satisfaction" as well as "joy." *Etre à l'aise* is to feel at ease, at home, to lack tension, to be relaxed. Here the sense conveyed is of self-assurance, somewhat stronger than simply being relaxed. (Tr.)

society without more or less concrete changes to the means of culture in the form of language and images. For women to be respected, but also for them to respect one another among themselves, linguistic and representational contexts have to give them subjective rights and methods of mediation equivalent to those of men. Otherwise they are both subordinated to masculine identity, and that includes when they imagine themselves to have found self-assurance, and continuously encroaching upon one another for want of their own subjectivity.

I think you'll agree with me that these changes are necessary. Can you give an indication of how you are starting to bring them about in your teaching at the university?

L. M.:   Self-assurance, the being who is self-assured in the world, means: to be in the world, no longer foreign or enslaved to it, but as women (*donne, dominae:* ladies, mistresses) to feel at home and secure in oneself. In order to attain this control, without basing it on means of domination such as money and arms, changes have to be made, and particularly at the symbolic level, as you have emphasized.

The following simple observation makes clear that the need for these changes has resurfaced negatively: after twenty years of a women's liberation movement that is still flourishing, many people still understand it as women's wish to be equal to men. This is a false interpretation. But it's *probable,* given that it fits in with the dominant paradigms in all fields: from politics, where "equal opportunity" is now all the rage, to religion, where female ordination is understood by those for and against it as a right demanded by women in relation to men and not as a social need for females to be social mediators, which some women feel called to do in the form of religious ministry.

I'm working for the changes you mention by combating this systematic deformation of female will. I don't fight it when it's the work of men; I'd rather leave this task to others, men or women. I'm better placed to combat it when it's simmering in the female brain (spirit?); I'm using bellicose language on purpose. Sometimes the theory of difference actually awakens a sort of crossfire in the female spirit between the desire for liberty and the fear of conflict with men, between a desire to separate from men and a fear of autonomy. The means I deploy in this struggle, those that suit me best, are not direct operations on language and on symbolic systems in general, though I do support them, as I think they're important. The means I prefer are social practices capable of giving women strength, such as the *affidamento* ("entrustment"),[7] the practice of difference, separate female communities, homosexuality. This is the direction I'm working in at the university, to produce all the strength we need to conquer probability with the aim of being able to know and speak the truth.

L. I.:   So the liberation of women leaves us with no choice other than to take this decisive and significant step: the interpretation of culture as a liberating, or oppressive and exploitative, means of production. Would you agree with this political analysis? Our objective, then, is not equality in the possession of material goods alone. What has to be won over also concerns justice and spiritual well-being. What do you

---

[7] Relationship of trust between two women, in which the younger asks the elder to help her to obtain something she desires.

92

think about this? Aside from your teaching, can you suggest other ways you can make this new History happen, in which there will no longer be a division between economy in the strict sense and cultural economy?

L. M.:   You've raised a theme that's too broad and too significant for me to deal with in the little space we have here. In pursuing this path we are, as you know, following on from Simone Weil. No one that I know of has as yet given as much thought as she did to how to link the material economy to the economy of spiritual goods. Among those who have gone before us, I think we also have to mention Enrico Berlinguer, who proposed years ago (but without any success) a change in political direction along the lines you suggest.

We can, indeed we must, continue where this research left off. We have something else, too, to help us: the political women's movement. Within women's politics there are some aspects that go beyond economism, such as the strengthening of subjectivity, the consideration given to qualitative differences, the recognition of the significance of the symbolic. Aside from all that, there is female experience—located outside the structures of economism—which could be beneficial to us, provided that it is transformed from within into knowledge and social capabilities.

On the last question, as to the means, I can't give an answer because I want to give it further thought.

January 1988

93

12

YOUR HEALTH

What, or Who, Is It?

How can women's health be defined? Hardly anything, in our present society, enables women to be *female sexed subjects* . . . So what is a possible definition of their well-being? They are often slightly unwell? Maybe. How could this be otherwise when there's no space for a woman's self-affirmation as I (*je*), but when, on the contrary, we must continuously support the assertions of others: in discourse, in images, in actions, and particularly in the commercial use of the self. Even if, on the whole, our societies no longer expect girls to have a dowry, the sale of female bodies has not declined on the art and industrial markets, and in advertising and the media: commerce that has the backing of the state and meets with silence from religious and moral authorities.

Female health raises another issue that is very difficult to resolve. How can the natural suffering a woman experiences during childbirth be separated from the artificial suffering society imposes upon her? I think most women still experience childbirth alone,[1] that no one allows them to talk about it as *subjects*, but rather they are always valorized as *mothers*, and thus as having suffered. They are identified as such and pass on this identity they bear as a *talion*: to be a woman, you must suffer.

BECOMING A WOMAN: WITHOUT SUFFERING

A young Italian friend of mine recently confided in me that she thinks all mothers are a little spiteful. She had been intimidated and hurt while working with older women, almost all of them mothers. There's some truth in what she says. I won't term this phallocracy—which would be once again to justify sexual indifferentiation by applying male models of interpretation to women. I think it's more the result of what right to existence society accords to women who have suffered giving birth. From women's point of view, I would call it a one-way ordeal. Women don't make the return journey, or at least most of them don't. They make others pay for it, like the initiated who have been slightly or greatly traumatized. What's more, most of the time women only make contact with each other in the context of discussions concerning their children, and mothers and daughters only ever come together, in our cultures, once they've passed the entrance test for the mother's clan.

---

[1] Not to mention their loss of virginity, and indeed most sexual relations, which are clothed in even more secrecy and which for many women are a physical and spiritual ordeal owing to the lack of a culture of sexuality.

Of course, motherhood does bring women a good deal of happiness. But this is conditional upon a great amount of pain, acknowledged to be one of the greatest forms of physical suffering it is possible to bear. If this becomes the norm for becoming a woman, then the suffering of childbirth justifies suffering in sexual relationships, the moral suffering of women, etc., which is all reinforced by their "masochism" and their capacity to endure. It's true to say that our present culture still doesn't leave them with many other options. Masochists are those who turn aggression meant for others against themselves. Should women, in turn, be aggressive, too?

But is this definition, originally a male one, suitable for us? Or should we think about a different female identity, in which the sufferings and joys of motherhood are no longer the criteria for identification?

Women cope fairly well with the suffering of childbirth if they choose to be pregnant or if "other" women help them to talk about the experience, which in many respects is difficult. But if motherhood is forced upon them as their inescapable fate, following on from some "original sin," then it becomes an unbearable injustice for women: the deprivation of their subjective rights.

Defining an adult woman almost exclusively in terms of motherhood stirs up an excessive amount of interest in discoveries related to artificial methods of procreation. Too much fuss is made about this, and too much money is channeled into it. There are plenty of other problems for us to deal with at present, especially concerning women's status, without concentrating on one more child for a sterile couple. Forgive me, all those suffering this ordeal! But there are many children looking for natural or spiritual parents. If having children is an act of generosity, then here's a chance to show it.

Of course, artificial procreation does raise a good number of scientific and ethical questions. In this respect, we can't be indifferent to it. And occasionally, it does have the advantage of making clear that sterility isn't only a woman's problem, as people believed for many years and some still do. I also think that, among other things, scientists sense in this, whether consciously or not, a way of overcoming God the creator, while some women see it as a way to rid themselves of the need for men. All these ways of destabilizing a given social model are being carried through too hastily, without clear-sightedness and without the affirmation or establishment of better values. They are being carried out, too, at the expense of those little children whose need, above all, is to be born into a habitable world. It wouldn't be a bad thing, nowadays, if we improved the conditions of natural and spiritual life so as to deal with procreation in a reasonable manner. It seems to me that one of the spiritual tasks for our time is to ask ourselves what the future holds for existing children rather than blindly jumping on the bandwagon of having them. Learning to like your self, your sex, the other sex, their particular or common creations—isn't this what we need at the very least to reach some sense, socially, here and now?

THOUGHT AS MEDICINE

For a while now schools have taught adolescents about sexuality by way of laboratory methods of procreation that make these future lovers disgusted with love and themselves. When will we teach them about love, exactly? Love that can't be reduced to the analysis of a reproductive genital mechanism but concerns the emotions between at least two people. When will we have literature lessons involving such things as "A

———

97

letter to my boyfriend or girlfriend"? Or art lessons imagining and creating an outline or face of a dream lover? Or photographic exhibitions at school of girls or boys who are close friends, who are lovable or loved? Love may perhaps require secrecy, but it also needs culture and a social context in order to last and develop. So when will we have words and images taught in our schools enabling and helping love to be? This would be so simple to do and would cost so little! Such progress is necessary for the development of the human order, progress that women and adolescents particularly need, as it has been denied them for centuries. But men need it too, and everyone can contribute—to a greater or lesser extent—to this social transformation in which the pleasure principle will have more chance than death drives, to use the terminology of Freud and Marcuse.

I think women's health suffers above all from their lack of self-affirmation and from the impossibility of or denial of a definition of women as subjects and objects by and for themselves. They are deprived of a subjective order by which they can unify their corporeal vitality. A body can only be sound if it has a personal or spiritual project or objective, keeping it together and bringing it to life. Without this dimension, it is bound to be ill, ill in many ways, unable to keep itself together, with no suitable medical cure. Resorting to an exclusively somatic treatment might well give it even less chance of true healing.

To be in good health, women need to discover for themselves the characteristics of their sexed identity. They also need reciprocity in sexual difference, whether it's a question of love, culture, society, or politics. Humanity is comprised of two different subjective identities and their respective objects or objectives. It's profoundly pathological and pathogenic for subjective and objective rights to be so unequally distributed. What can help women to "get over" this is an initiation into subjectivity. At the very least this requires an understanding of the scale of the problem, friendship and mutual respect to attempt to resolve it, a thorough cultural critique, and, sometimes, recourse to psychotherapy. Which is why we have to train therapists who are able to help women!

February 1988

13

HOW CAN WE CREATE OUR BEAUTY?

Very often, when looking at women's works of art, I have been saddened by the sense of anguish they express, an anguish so strong it approaches horror. Having wanted to contemplate beauty created by women, I would find myself faced instead with distress, suffering, irritation, sometimes ugliness. The experience of art, which I expected to offer a moment of happiness and repose, of compensation for the fragmentary nature of daily life, of unity and communication or communion, would become yet another source of pain, a burden.

I wondered why women exhibit such pain and agony, women I believe to be more than capable of creating beauty. I thought over some of the reasons why. I'd like to express what I think so as to help women exteriorize in their works of art the beauty, and the forms of beauty, of which they are capable.

1. I am one of these women. And although I do avoid writing about and pointing to things that are wretched, ugly, I often have occasion to deal with painful realities. As far as I'm able, I discuss them in a literary style, which I hope cushions the sense of dereliction these disclosures can lead to. I also strive to discover or define something positive at the same time I'm stating the negative. I am, moreover, criticized for this, by women among others, who have a tendency to identify only with what they lack, their shortcomings.

   Personally, I rather regret having to show the negative, but the point of doing it, from a female perspective, is positive and necessary given that it reveals what was meant to remain hidden.

   The portrayal of suffering is, then, for women an act of truthfulness. It's also akin to an individual and collective catharsis. As women they've been obliged to keep quiet about what they go through, and have often converted it into physical symptoms, mutism, paralysis, etc. Daring to manifest publicly individual and collective pain has a therapeutic effect, bringing relief to the body and enabling them to accede to another time. This doesn't come as a matter of course, but it may be the case for some women, for the female people. The anguish shown in women's works might be related to those masked characters of Greek tragedy who were subject to the force of fate. Some would be overdressed, particularly as women, others completely stripped, denuded. No longer would they have even their skin intact to keep them together physically, no longer even the love of their mother to protect their identity as girls, as virgins.

2. As women, we engender children. Can one create anything more extraordinary, bodily or spiritually, than a living being? This creation, which is our preserve, is so wonderful that all other works can seem secondary, even raising the children themselves. But this marvelous women's work has been turned into an obligation to procreate, especially boys. The greatest creators of the universe, women, have thus become servants devoted to the reproduction of the male social order. Of all the glory of their greatest work, often all they keep is the pain of the "labor" of childbirth and the trials of mothering. On top of this, the patriarchal cultural order has reduced them to what's labeled procreation by forbidding them to be creative or making it impossible for them to do so. As far as childbirth goes, there would seem to be confusion nowadays between the beauty of the work and its definition within a between-men civilization in which women no longer have a recognized right to engender spiritual values.

3. As women, we have thus been enclosed in an order of forms inappropriate to us. In order to exist, we must break out of these forms. That act of liberation from imposed norms could have various results:

   (a) It may be that, in wanting to throw off the physical and spiritual clothing of oppression, we destroy ourselves, too. Instead of being reborn, we annihilate ourselves.

   (b) Or, in breaking out of our formal prisons, our shackles, we may discover what flesh we have left. I think color is what's left of life beyond forms, beyond truth or beliefs, beyond accepted joys and sorrows. Color also expresses our sexuate nature, that irreducible dimension of our incarnation (cf. "Les Couleurs de la chair" in *Sexes et parentés*). When all meaning is taken away from us, there remains color, colors, in particular those corresponding to our sex. Not the dullness of the neuter, the non-living or problematically living (stones, for example) but the colors that are ours owing to the fact that we are women. Colors are also present in nature—particularly plant life— and there they express life, its becoming and its development according to days, seasons, years. In the world around us, they also express what is sexuate in life.

(c) Or, finally, it may be that in destroying already coded forms, women rediscover their nature, their identity, and are able to find their forms, to blossom out in accordance with what they are. Furthermore, these female forms are always incomplete, in perpetual growth, because a woman grows, blossoms, and fertilizes (herself) within her own body. But she cannot be reduced to a single flower, as in the male image of virginity. In line with her own virginity, she is never completed in a single form. She is ceaselessly becoming, she "flowers" again and again, if she stays close to herself and the living world.

4. The between-men cultures have deprived us of the expression of meaning through images, which for the most part constitutes our female and maternal genius. The child a woman engenders is visible in a multitude of moving and

developing images. It is not an abstract nor arbitrary sign. For us women, meaning remains concrete, close, related to what is natural, to perceptible forms. It also develops like our bodies, those of our children, of our sexual partners, of those that belong to the living world. At that time in History—conventionally termed Prehistory—when women participated in civil and religious life, written signs were still partially figurative, non-abstract, arbitrary, fiduciary. In those days women were represented as goddesses: not only as mother-goddesses—the only ones subsequent eras accepted—but also as women-goddesses. This is particularly evident in the fact that women-goddesses are beautiful, slim, and their sex marked by a triangle (as for mother-goddesses) in which the lips are drawn; all this was to be wiped out by what followed. Their divinity doesn't depend upon the fact they can be mothers but upon their female identity, of which the half-open lips are an affirmative expression.

The loss of divine representation has brought women to a state of dereliction, which is felt all the more because sensible representation is our primary method of figuration and communication. It has left us without a means of designating ourselves, of expressing ourselves, between ourselves. It has also separated mothers from daughters, depriving them of mutually respectful mediums of exchange. It has subjected them to a reproductive order—natural and spiritual—that is governed symbolically by men.

In my view we can and must rediscover the originality of our works. They are particularly important for sensible representations of ourselves, of our world, of vertical and horizontal relations between ourselves. Of course, this creativity correlates to what our current world—gray, abstract and destitute—needs. Even if it is reluctant to recognize our work as being necessary, we can and must accomplish it as a woman's and a mother's contribution to not only the natural but also the spiritual life of the world. With this intention, the beauty of our works is a medium that enables us to pass from nature to the spirit, while all the while remaining natural. Isn't that where our genius lies?

March 1988

14

HOW OLD ARE YOU?

How old are you? This seems to be a dreaded question in our cultures, in which age signifies getting old. Growing older means adding one more year to your age. Therefore, apart from the few years of growing up, aging is always a matter of getting old from an accumulation of years, and from increasing organic waste or decay.

"How old are you?" is a question that should hardly ever be put to a woman, for example, for risk of offending her. Because it would seem she's only lovable or desirable in her youth, or for other reasons, during her childbearing years.

What can we make of this conception of age? There are at least two considerations missing from it:

1. The relationship between how old I am and the time of the universe. One year of my life consists of a spring, a summer, an autumn, and a winter. During these seasons, many

things happen which cannot be reduced to one. Neither days, nor seasons, nor years are alike. And their progress can't be confused with a simple addition. If you look at a tree, you'll see that, in one year, its shape will have changed, not simply from decline but also from growth— its size, the number of branches, etc. What humans have, besides the vegetative, is consciousness. Their growth, their development could also be spiritual. Assisted by the seasons, we might bring about, every year, a new becoming, as a continuation of, but different from, that of the previous year. Being a year older would thus mean being a little further on the way to one's future becoming.

Obviously, the fact of living in an urban landscape accustoms us to forgetting this sense of time with which the vegetable world presents us. In cities, daily timetables vary very little, whatever the season. Apart from Sundays and holidays, urban rhythms remain more or less the same throughout the year. What's more, the use of industrialized or imported food products also helps us to forget the temporality of the days, seasons, and years. In this sense, one year = 365 or 366 days, and being a year older amounts to having accumulated repeated hours, days, and years that are all very similar.

Repetition without progression is wearisome, exhausting, and damaging. It's as if every birthday marks a stage of this futureless becoming, or else a fairly abstract sum of facts that are practically devoid of sense and continuity. The individual celebrating her or his birthday no longer holds the key to understanding these facts. Part of it is to found in the commercial economy, which individuals more often than not put up with even if they don't find much pleasure in it all.

———

2. It is forgotten that time in a woman's life is particularly irreversible, and that, compared to men's time, it is less suited to the repetitive, entropic, and largely non-progressive, nullifying economy of our present environment. In fact, this economy's temporal rhythm more or less accords with a traditional model of male sexuality. It's not the only model possible, but it has just about become so in our cultures; Freud described it as the only sexual model for both sexes. It operates according to the two principles of thermodynamics: tension (by accumulation), discharge, return to homeostasis.

Female sexuality does not correspond to the same economy. It is more related to becoming, more attuned to the time of the universe.

Which means that a woman's life can't be reduced to a series of facts or activities that can be added up or taken away. A woman's life is marked by irreversible events that define the stages of her life. This is true for puberty (which boys also experience), losing her virginity, becoming pregnant, being pregnant, childbirth, breastfeeding—events that can be repeated without repetition: each time, they happen differently: body and spirit have changed, physical and spiritual development is taking place. There are also mothering and bringing up young children, which a woman is more involved with, leaving her constantly in touch with problems of growth and development. During all this time, a woman experiences menstruation, her periods, as continuously related to cosmic time, to the moon, the sun, the tides, and the seasons.

Finally, menopause marks another stage in the becoming of a female body and spirit, a stage characterized by a different hormonal equilibrium, another relation to the

---

cosmic and the social. What is often defined as the end of a woman's life is for her just as much an opportunity to have more time for social, cultural, and political life.

A birthday can't, therefore, be reduced to an addition of one more year, to a sort of non-progressive if not negative sum. This is especially true for women. Nothing in their lives resembles an accumulation of 1 + 1 + 1 ... unless they renounce their nature. They are, due to the fact of having a female body, in perpetual growth, and that includes during the final part of their life.

To go through the aging process as if it were just a question of getting old amounts to forgetting what an opportunity it is to have been born female, an opportunity that, granted, requires of us a multiple and complex spiritual development. Indeed, a little girl's spirituality is not the same as an adolescent's, nor a lover's, nor a mother's, nor that of a woman of forty-five or older. Perhaps it's the complexity of this spiritual becoming that has brought about the severe reduction of female identity to the function of reproducer of the individual, species, and society. This subjective reduction, simplification, and denial go hand in hand with cultural development centered on exchanges between men, notably economic ones in the strict sense. They are encouraged, at least in modern times, by monotheistic religions.

How can we get out of this subjective paralysis or annihilation? How can we keep and develop a female identity?

What I've found to be most important to sustain spiritual progress in my life as a woman can be summarized in the following way:

1. The idea that I was born a woman but I must become the

spirit or soul of this body I am. I must open out my female body, give it forms, words, knowledge of itself, a cosmic and social equilibrium, in relation to the environment, to the different means of exchange with others, and not only by artificial means that are inappropriate to it.

2. The idea that virginity and maternity involve spiritual dimensions that belong to me. These dimensions have been colonized by masculine culture: virginity has become the object of commerce between fathers (or brothers) and husbands, as well as a condition for the incarnation of the masculine divine. It has to be rethought as a woman's possession, a natural and spiritual possession to which she has a right and for which she holds responsibilities.

Virginity must be rediscovered by all women as their own bodily and spiritual possession, which can give them back an individual and collective identity status (and, among other things, a possible fidelity in their relationship with their mother, which would thereby escape the commerce between men). Maternity must be thought of in its spiritual dimension, not only its material one. This is perhaps easier to imagine and carry out. Though not between mothers and daughters?

Women must develop a double identity: virgins and mothers. At every stage of their lives. Since virginity, no more than female identity, isn't simply given at birth. There's no doubt we are born virgins. But we also have to become virgins, to relieve our bodies and souls of cultural and familial fetters. For me, becoming a virgin is synonymous with a woman's conquest of the spiritual. And it's not always a matter of gaining something more but one of being capable of something less. Feeling more free vis-à-vis your fears, fantasies about others, freeing yourself from useless knowledge, possessions, and obligations.

A lifetime isn't too long to make this happen! Growing older can help us to do it by crossing frontiers that then leave us more free to get on with accomplishing our identity.

April 1988

15

THE COST OF WORDS

Although the issue of pay, of fair or adequate renumeration at work, has in recent years received considerable attention, very little attention has been given to the economic context in the broader sense to which pay applies. In this piece I will approach this issue from within the framework of sexual difference; that is: What is the relationship between language and work in the strict sense as far as sexual difference is concerned?

There's no longer any need to repeat, or at least I hope there isn't, that the ideal of "equal pay for equal work" is far from being achieved between men and women, and that the discrepancy between payment and work can go so far as to turn pay norms on their head, so that for more difficult work, for longer hours, for better work, the pay is less. There is thus a sexist ideology in force in the economy in the strict sense, most of the time unconscious. It is conveyed by language. It's not merely a given fact of nature, as those who are culturally naive would have us believe so as to perpetuate the current state of affairs. What we have here are the structures of a socially constructed division of labor that continues to operate in the guise of apparently pure economism. Women shall perform reproductive and unpaid domestic labor, men paid productive work—these categories are still at work in what is taken to be self-evident or at least partial social progress. This way of defining work, with this suitable for women and that for men, is far from being a simple fact of physical nature, and what's more, there are no grounds for paying less for one body's work than for another's. We should have learned such truths from all the antiracist struggles, even if women find it difficult to have to cite this example to make themselves understood. Yet sexism is the most unconscious form of racism and gives rise to a multitude of contradictions before revealing itself. Hence:

1. Men are the creators and take themselves to be the driving force behind most of our present culture; nevertheless, in most cases women teach this, because teaching is likened to the work of a mother and is therefore left to women and as a result is underpaid.[1]
2. If a woman is a good worker—as is said to be the case— accepting the fact that she might need several months off to have a child doesn't cost a firm a great deal compared to her usual input, and dismissing her is an irrational act in economic terms.
3. The use of physical strength as an argument to bolster

---

[1] Cf. *Lettera di una professoressa*, paper published by the feminist section of the Italian Communist Party's national committee.

male pay meets with many contradictions in reality: women's presence in the agricultural sector where physical strength is a requirement, the increasing development of production methods that require little physical strength, the sort of work women carry out in other cultures.

There are numerous examples of irrationality to be found in the way pay is awarded for work, and they are on the increase. The fact that such irrationality continues to be implemented suggests that a disguised form of violence is being used in what passes for social order.

The force or strength of ideology within the economy in the strict sense has a bearing upon the following:

1. Recruitment for women's jobs and men's jobs; the redundancy levels for each sex and the reasons given for them, not to mention the unions' differing response in each case; the percentage of unemployed, which varies according to sex. In terms of profit and loss, nothing justifies such criteria of choice on the part of employers. The female workforce is generally more conscientious and efficient. They drink less, take fewer drugs, and overall are less likely to commit offenses leading to criminal convictions. Why does an employer choose against his own best interests?

2. Positions open to women. The fact of being a woman puts a ceiling on professional qualification. Women are very largely concentrated in those sectors of employment needing few qualifications. Those who reach the highest positions are rare indeed, and some pay dearly for it; either they accept that they must prostitute themselves in one way or another in order to obtain a more senior post, or

they have to renounce their female qualities so as to be thought suitable for a particular position (thus, it is not as women that they succeed).

3. The way occupations largely comprised of women are devalued, no matter how significant they are for social production and reproduction, in the agricultural, industrial, and cultural sectors.

To all that, one may add further important considerations regarding the work context:

1. The laws of work organization are still generally determined by men, and women have to adapt to them. But it's possible to show that these laws are just as biased towards cultural values that haven't been thought out as they are to production imperatives. Work hours are a good example of how organizations typically favor a male workforce with a woman at home, doing the domestic chores and looking after the children. Likewise, without going into the problems presented by child care—which are never solved by chore-sharing between men and women—grocery stores are open in many areas while the woman is at work, so she can't do the shopping. Another example: the fact that plumbers and electricians work at the same time as everyone else, and their hours assume a housewife at home. Or again: some industries have set night shifts. Of course, it's only fair for women to have the right to work at night if they so desire, and the use of child care as blackmail affects fathers as much as mothers. But is this night work really helping to solve humanity's present or future problems, or does it arise out of problems of economic competitiveness, which are secondary in relation to

the social problems to be solved, especially those issues of difference between the sexes?[2]

2. Ideas and decisions about what should be produced are still usually subject to male authority. If it's agreed that the right to work is one of our basic needs and an essential element of human dignity, why should one part of humanity be subject to the other's choices when it comes to the nature of production? Take, for example, arms production, continuing or increased pollution, the glut of useless products on the market: these are rarely the result of decisions made by women. Their choices tend more toward maintaining peace, a clean environment, goods we really need in life, humanitarian options. The issues at stake in the choices of financial groups or military blocs, such as a wish for supremacy over currency or over another country, are quite foreign to women. Similarly, the proliferation of products for the purpose of economic competitiveness signifies a sort of commerce that is of little interest to women. Which doesn't mean that they are incapable of it, especially through mimicry or indoctrination by advertising, but rather that they prefer production that meets everyone's needs. Another example: the choice of leisure activities available, and more specifically the media, feed into a between-men culture. Male sport is all-pervasive, and television stations don't hesitate in replacing a cultural program aimed at both sexes with a football match. Women, however, pay the same as men to enjoy television programs (not to mention the thousands,

[2] On this matter, see the working papers of the women of the Italian Communist Party: *La carta itinerante* (1986), *Il tempo delle donne* (1988), *Le donne cambiano i tempi* (1990).

raised from both sexes' taxes, invested in building all sorts of sports stadiums). But they are not the target audience. Male fantasies, on the other hand, find daily fulfillment in military, pornographic, and violent films that are of absolutely no interest to women. Therefore, there is a gap between the price paid and the product being offered, true for both public and private services. This economic injustice in the strict sense is reinforced by policies maintaining the illusion of egalitarianism. Which means that nowadays, in schools, in the media, etc., women maintain the discourse of their alienation. In order to get a job, for example, they teach that the universal is masculine, that the masculine is more valuable, that the percentage of great men in History is infinitely superior to that of great women. They don't choose what they teach because they aren't in the management posts that would enable them to make such decisions. In order to earn their living, they are held hostage to the between-men economy and culture, which has nothing universal about it, other than by wiping out sexual difference. Women, when they are allowed into systems of social production, therefore work in conditions that do not respect them as persons in the physical and moral senses (the right to motherhood, to acceptable hours of work, to a job compatible with their bodies and their identities).

3. Codes of conduct within the workplace are nearly all laid out in accordance with natural languages valorizing a male subject, either explicitly or implicitly, in the content or style of the prevalent discourses (military discourse plays an important role). Women are not paid for the physical, psychic, and intersubjective effect this between-men culture has on them, and it's not even recognized or

———

considered. Yet all you have to do is carry out studies aimed at appraising, in quantitative as well as qualitative terms, the development of female identity subject to an exclusively masculine cultural ambiance, in order to get an idea of the price they pay. I have already carried out or coordinated a number of studies on this subject, with an emphasis on language (in different languages). I am continuing this work, in collaboration with others, by extending the study to other domains: love, health, family relations, cultural relations, etc.[3] The price women must pay to enter fields managed by men proves to be quite similar to that currently paid by all workers who are subject to a language that is foreign to them: in computing, for example. In Italy, intellectuals working for unions and therapists have organized discussion groups to analyze this. These discussion groups on new technologies have brought to the fore the effects of using a linguistic code foreign to the self: progressive isolation, the fragmentary nature of knowledge, the "flight of knowledge" through its management by computers rather than oneself (or male bosses?). All these cause feelings of anguish and aggression, and a progressive loss of identity. Feelings are sometimes so strong that it can be difficult or even impossible for collective opinions or a working group to be formed. Isolation is taken to be a way of behaving, of thinking, as an inter- or intra-subjective mechanism; this gives an impression of the defenses male and female workers need, subjected to codes they cannot master.[4] Those who claim

[3] Cf. *Sexes et genres à travers les langues, op. cit.*, and "L'ordre sexuel de la langue et du discours" (handout from my course at the International College of Philosophy, 1988–89).

[4] Cf. Working paper of the Clinica psichiatrica, University of Bologna.

---

this occurs only in other countries and not in ours should spend a couple of days in the company of workers who have to use computers: railway staff (S.N.C.E), post office staff (P.T.T.). These public sector workers no longer know how to be polite or what their own interests are. You need only ask them for something (which you're paying for) and they will be lecturing you, insulting you, even though their failure to master their work makes them incompetent. The mounting aggression of these workers, who are social mediators, gives us good cause to worry; it is aggressiveness resulting from the changes brought about in their work through the use of a computer, with a screen intervening between themselves and the customer.

Working can't simply be reduced to earning money. Work has human value, individual and collective human value. This is conveyed in various ways. The sort of work and the way it's carried out is one of them; another is the way the work is valorized by its social designation. The way in which a worker can relate to the goods produced is a third. A fourth is how the worker, as an individual, and his or her product appear in advertising and the media. There are plenty of others.

The following three examples show how unequally male and female labor is valorized, and thus how unequal forms of payment reward their labor:

1. *Occupational status*: unequally accessible but also unequally rewarding for the two sexes. Indeed, being valorized at work isn't simply a function of salary increases. Among other things, it's expressed by a change in the title designating professional level. And in that, too, the norms and shortcomings of linguistic codes and customs, their

resistance to change, makes it difficult to designate occupational status for women. This issue has been dealt with often, as it represents an intermediary space between subject and object, worker and salary. In addition, it is a demand that takes up, or easily fits in with, already existing demands in the male world of work. It is therefore easier to state the objective. But possible solutions meet with obstacles in the form of already existing linguistic codes (so *médecine*, for example, designates a means or a discipline in the professional life of a *médecin*, or the female of the word designating the profession is pejorative owing to its suffix: *doctoresse*[5] and social resistance as to which professional levels should be accessible to women. Which can cause, along with a great deal of social injustice, quite amusing and strange linguistic facts or anomalies.[6]

2. *The designation of objects and goods:* Female subjects and their professional qualities are still poorly represented in linguistic terms. And it is impossible, in the Romance languages, to equalize the value of the feminine through the conquest of goods or objects, because difference between the sexes isn't immediately shown by the relation to the possessed object in Italian or in French as it is in English or German, for example. The possessive takes, in the former languages, the object's gender and not the possessor's. One says: he or she travels in *sa* car; he or she kisses *son*

[5] *Médicin* means doctor; here, adding an "e" to form the feminine doesn't produce a term applicable to a female subject: *médicine* refers to a medical practice, to medicine. (Tr.)

[6] Irigaray cites the example of an obituary in the newspaper *L'indépendant*, 3 September 1987, of a politician and economist, Nicole Chouraqui, and refers the reader to her analysis of this in "Comment devenir des femmes civiles?" in *Le Temps de la Différence* (Paris: Biblio Essais, 1989).

child; he or she is writing *son* book in *sa* house. And if an Anglo-Saxon woman can be satisfied with her (*sa*) husband (and he with his (*son*) wife), having bought her (*sa*) house, with having obtained her (*sa*) university post, having written her (*sa*) book, etc., it doesn't work the same for women whose language is much more sedimented in terms of subjectivity. This signifies that subject-object relations are much more complex in Romance languages, and that things and words themselves have sexed properties as do subjects.[7]

Today it has become fashionable to say that the gender of words is arbitrary, that it bears no relation to the question of sex. This is incorrect. The gender of words is, in one way or another, related to the question of the gender of speaking subjects. Words have, so to speak, a hidden sex, and this sex is valorized unequally according to whether it is male or female. It is a fact not always immediately obvious, and often in-depth studies, synchronic and diachronic, on the lexicon and the syntax of a language have to be undertaken to make it apparent.

There is another mechanism at work in addition to the identification of designated reality and sex:

(a) living beings, animate, human, cultured, become masculine;
(b) lifeless objects, inanimate, non-human, uncultured, become feminine.

Which means that only men become social subjects and that women are assimilated to objects of exchange between them. This status of word gender gradually

[7] See also 8. "Linguistic Sexes and Genders," p. 60, and *Sexes et Genres à Travers les Langues*, "Conclusions," *op. cit.*

developed with patriarchal cultures, defined by their exchange of women between men, the domination of the family by the father and patrilinearity (or the avuncular matrilineal structure which preceded it), the appropriation by the man-father of goods: land, tools, the home, arts, languages, gods, the sky, etc. The patriarch thus possesses women and tools as goods that are often denoted by the feminine gender. This is one of the reasons why naming occupations for women is so often a problem: the feminine of the masculine term has become the gender of the thing used by the man. For example, *le moissoneur* (harvester) is a man, *la moissonneuse* (harvesting machine) is his tool, *le médecin* (doctor) is a man, *la médecine* (medicine) is his tool, etc.[8] There is therefore a triple difficulty in using these words to name a woman's occupational status:

(a) Men are attached to their tools' sex, which stands in for their sexual partners.
(b) Women don't want to be designated by a word that is denigrating to them as persons, and what is offered them is the name of a thing (*médecine*) or the name of a person with a pejorative suffix (*doctoresse*, for example).
(c) How can we put a woman to work with a tool that is her substitute?

These issues concerning language and socioeconomic status are complex. Once again, women find themselves penalized for being women in the present culture, which manifests a fundamental injustice with respect to their human identity.

3. *Advertising practices*, those of the media included, concerning

[8] See again 8. "Linguistic Sexes and Genders," p. 60. (Tr.)

products "for sale." Just as women have been exchange objects between men, families, or tribes, competitive sales techniques make authoritative use of their bodies and speech without a care for their human dignity, working women included. Women are thus doubly devalued or exploited in the sense that they are used to sell products that perhaps they themselves have made.[9] What's more, advertisements typically present them as having a scornful attitude toward other women.

The cost of words, the economic meaning of discourse, discourses, constitutes one of the important problems of our time. There are many reasons for this. I'll give just five of them:

1. Women going out to work
2. The growing awareness of the meaning of economic justice
3. The tendency of our times to evaluate everything in figures
4. The movement toward artificial languages, particularly out of concern for profit, of demands to go "faster"
5. The subjection of natural languages and artificial codes to the reign of the consumable object and commercial exchange, with a significant loss of means of exchange, particularly reciprocal exchange, between individuals.

Relationships between people constitute one of the main areas of women's work, whether it's the work of being a mother, family work, teaching, caring for the sick, social work,

[9] The replies given to women protesting against advertising practices from the bodies responsible for them are themselves worthy of further study.

123

working as an air hostess, even secretarial work, etc. Curiously enough, this work, very specifically human, is still either unpaid or underpaid. Must interpersonal relations—of which women are the objective guardians in modern times—be seen as priceless? As having to remain unpaid? Because they are under- or overvalued? Unfortunately, our current culture responds by devaluing this work socially, too. Thus, teachers, nurses, social workers, or housewives are today demanding respect for their persons and for their work just as much as they are demanding salary increases (which is a tactic women often use).

Why is such work devalued to such an extent? Is it because it's female work or because it concerns relationships between people, and not the production and selling of objects? These two factors may coincide, but they do raise important questions for the present and for the future of human culture. Are we forgetting the cost of language as a means of communication between people? Are we losing our humanity to manufactured objects, to which we are becoming enslaved, or in favor of purely financial exchanges, to which we are servants? Are we already so enslaved by machines that we have lost our freedom of choice in many situations? What is, then, the meaning of speech in our time? And if we no longer speak, speak to each other, are we still human? Are we still alive? This issue seems to coincide with the lack of concern for the passage from nature to culture when it comes to our sexed identity, and with the small price accorded to intersubjective relations, which are more related to the personal and to women's work.

May 1989

———

16

SO WHEN ARE WE TO BECOME WOMEN?

Motherhood is back in fashion with women, some radical women included, especially because of artificial methods of fertilization. Will the new technologies get the better of female identity just as the old patriarchs did? The situation may be even worse. Indeed, the establishment of patriarchal power was not achieved without war, struggle, and murder, as anyone can see. You have only to look at History or PreHistory—just before the aforesaid History—to see this.[1]

Now that women are, today, orphaned, without she-gods, goddesses, a divine mother of daughters, without a spiritual genealogy, they will do anything to assert a degree of independence, risking a further loss of female identity. Having a child without a man apparently represents the height of

---

[1] Cf., 2. "Religious and Civil Myths," p. 15.

liberty for some women. Yet this still amounts to defining oneself in relation to the other sex rather than oneself; it amounts to thinking of oneself without the other and not to thinking one's self, thinking about oneself, about myself as a woman (*à moi-elle*), about ourselves by our selves as women (*à nous et avec nous-elles*).

What's more, a child without a man is still a child. A woman will still always be the mother in this situation. And if women's liberation is defined exclusively by their ability to manage procreation without men, then it's a very precarious liberty, I think. Especially as the man is not absent from artificial procreation. He is present in at least three ways.

1. First, a child conceived without a male sexual partner nevertheless depends upon male semen. Now, is there any worse form of naturalism than this conception by anonymous semen, separated from the subject who produced it? Certain feminists, who rail passionately against relating women to their nature and to nature, thus fall back on the blueprint for biology drawn up by the male people: nature devoid of all grace, the emasculation of *female* desire.

2. Next, men are not at all absent from reproductive technologies. They have even taken a great interest in it for monetary reasons. Prostitution makes money out of women's sex; artificial procreation makes it out of the mother's womb.

3. Finally, it's the patriarchal world that has confined women to motherhood. And as long as women are concerned about their wombs, which always cause them to be slightly "unwell" according to Simone de Beauvoir— whom it would have been wise to ask why women's wombs should "naturally" make them unwell—that will be

---

their (only) concern. The social structure, political and religious authority, symbolic exchanges—in short, all serious spiritual things remain in the hands of men.

Today's scientists poring over their test tubes to decide a woman's fertility or fertilization very much resemble theologians speculating about the possibility of a female soul or about the point at which the fetus' soul comes into existence. The approach is similar, perhaps worse. And if need be, some of these scientists will be women. But this won't be enough to define female identity. Such technological changes in patriarchy seem quite trivial compared with the task women have—to make good a loss of identity that in all probability makes them sterile and sick. They are hardly ethical, either, insofar as they continue to draw attention to the production of yet one more child, without considering what is to become of this child in today's world and in the future. So some women previously unable to have children will be able to? Fine. But how many children nowadays are dying of natural or spiritual hunger? Why then all this fuss surrounding the possibility of motherhood? Because the framework for women's existence is exclusively maternal. And there's a real risk that some women, who think themselves freed from their nature such as it was defined by patriarchy, will once again subject themselves body and "soul" to this variant on their fate called artificial procreation.

Test-tube mothers, surrogate mothers, men engendering futuristically (in their intestines?): what next? Will all this help us get away from the pressure to have children, our sole sexual "vocation" according to the patriarchs, so as to get to know ourselves, to love and create ourselves in accordance with our bodily differences? I'm surprised that some radical women have embarked on such struggles while so many young women and so many girls expect their cultural elders to give them a lead on the possibility of their becoming women without an *exclusive* subjection to motherhood and without, for all that, being reduced to male identity. I think it shows that the goals of our liberation have remained tied to a culture that offers women no subjective opportunities, and that, for want of an identity of their own, many are, in a vague sort of way, trying to find a niche for themselves within a technological era that needs their energy to give itself the illusion of a future. It is sadly repetitive, wearisome, and rather discouraging, even if on the surface diverting attention in this way suits a good number of people . . .

INDEX

Heaven Is
Not My Home

HEAVEN IS
NOT MY HOME

Learning to Live in God's Creation

BY PAUL MARSHALL WITH LELA GILBERT

THOMAS NELSON PUBLISHERS
Nashville

Scripture references are from the following sources:

The Holy Bible, New International Version (NIV). Copyright © 1973, 1978, 1984, International Bible Society. Used by permission of Zondervan Bible Publishers.

The King James Version of the Bible (KJV).

The New King James Version (NKJV), copyright © 1979, 1980, 1982, 1992, Thomas Nelson, Inc., Publisher.

The New Jerusalem Bible (NJB). Copyright © 1990 by Doubleday & Co., Inc.

Special thanks to Calvin Seerveld for permission to quote extensively from his *Christian Workers of the World Unite!* and to Mike Starkey and Monarch Press for permission to quote extensively from his *Fashion and Style* (Crowborough: Monarch Press, 1995).

Library of Congress Cataloging-in-Publication Data
Marshall, Paul A., 1948–
   Heaven is not my home : learning to live in God's creation / by
Paul Marshall with Lela Gilbert.
     p. cm.
   Includes bibliographical references (p.).
   ISBN 0-8499-1471-X
   1. Christian life. I. Gilbert, Lela. II. Title.
   BV4501.2.M364325   1999
   261'.1—dc21

                 98-49520
                 CIP

Printed in the United States of America
8 9 0 1 2 3 4 5 BVG 9 8 7 6 5 4 3 2 1

CONTENTS

v

ACKNOWLEDGMENTS

This book has its beginning several years ago in conversations I had with Os Guinness and John Seel. I would like to thank them for their encouragement and enthusiasm—though they didn't know what would come out of it. Richard Mouw, Robert Banks, and Paul Stevens have taught me about the meaning of creation. The writings of Al Wolters on this theme have always inspired and, I think, shaped me. Mike Starkey's writings have shown me a little of what this means in some areas of life, and I will not soon forget the fashion show he put on in Doug and Ann Holt's church in London. I thank James and Wanda Coffey-Bailey, two people to whom I felt I could entrust the manuscript in its early stages: I thank them for their positive response. Ed Knipper's paintings have also shaped this book, and he and Diane Knipper's advice, encouragement, and hospitality were invaluable and much enjoyed. Howard and Robert Ahmanson have worked with these issues for many years: I hope they like what many passionate and delightful conversations with them have wrought.

If there is one person who has most shaped what I say here, it is my longtime colleague, mentor, and squash partner, Calvin Seerveld. I'm not sure if he will like all of what is here, but he is responsible for most of what is good here. The Institute for Christian Studies, at which I taught until very recently, provided an academic home and intellectually demanding environment. Last, but certainly not least, I want to thank Lela Gilbert, whose idea this book was, and who made it possible for me to write it.

———   🐦   ———

. . . We must come to a place where we comfortably think of God as a reality that is a part of our world. Until the church develops an understanding of the gospel that relates it more to this life than the next life, it will cause difficulties on both sides. Those on the outside of religion will look at it and regard it has having nothing to do with real life. Those on the inside of religion will experience their life outside of special religious activities as if it were a godless world. I think the key issue here lies deeper than even matters of integration as we commonly discuss it. It is a matter of our under-standing of the gospel of Jesus Christ as one which breaks through the natural world and brings in the spiritual world and invites us as individuals to learn to live an eternal kind of life now.

—Dallas Willard

PREFACE

You should know up front that this book is one-sided. The Bible portrays our world as *good*, destined for reunion with God in Jesus Christ. It is this *goodness* that I'll focus on here, and I make no apology for it. But the Bible also emphasizes the effects of sin on the world, and hence, creation's transitory character. Scripture teaches that God loves the world and cares for it (and always will), but also that we are sojourners in the present age. Here I have given much less attention to the second than the first.

This one-sidedness is quite deliberate. Unfortunately, among Christian believers, and especially among evangelicals, the theme of the goodness and permanence of the world is usually neglected, often forgotten, and sometimes denied entirely. Instead we are deluged with articles, books, sermons, and radio and TV programs warning us that the world, along with every human achievement, is going to be destroyed. This extreme position diminishes our place in God's world. Because of such misconceptions, many Christians today are, by and large, shirking their divinely given responsibility to sustain, nurture, renew, and really *live* in God's world.

Throughout the text are descriptive "snapshots" intended to give some glimpses of the wonders of living in God's creation. Although all of the stories are true, I have changed the names of most of the characters for the sake of privacy and protection.

This book is merely an attempt to give a brief overview of our *spiritual orientation* as we live as God's people in God's world. It gives few practical guidelines. There are no keys or twelve-step programs here. There is, however, a deep and heartfelt appeal that I hope will challenge what we think and believe about the world. The gospel calls for it. The Church needs it. And our world is literally dying for it.

This is my Father's world,
O let me ne'er forget
That though the wrong seems oft so strong,
God is the ruler yet.
This is my Father's world:
The battle is not done;
Jesus who died shall be satisfied,
And earth and heav'n be one.
—Maltbie D. Babcock

Our Fear
of the World

PART I